D1509021

ST. MARTIN'S GRIFFIN ≈ **NEW YORK**

AC/DC

THE WORLD'S HEAVIEST ROCK

Martin Huxley

[Frontispiece Photo: Fin Costello,
Redferns/Retna]

Design by Junie Lee

Library of Congress Cataloging-in-Publication Data

Huxley, Martin.
    AC/DC :   the world's heaviest rock / by Martin Huxley, —
1st St. Martin's Griffin ed.
        p.   cm.
    Discography: p.
    ISBN 0-312-14095-9
    1. AC/DC (Musical group)   2.Rock musicians—Australia—
Biography.   I. Title.
ML421.A28H8   1996
782.42166'092'2—dc20
[B]   95-41117
                                            CIP
                                            MN

First St. Martin's Griffin Edition: April 1996

10 9 8 7 6 5 4 3 2 1

The author would like to thank the following people for their contributions to this book: Jim Fitzgerald, Regan Good, Evie Greenbaum, Madeline Morel, Doug Wygal, David Fricke, Ira Robbins, Holly George-Warren, Dave and Regina Dunton, Maria Castello, Johnny Waller, Drew and Meryl Wheeler, Ken Weinstein, Deb Licis, Jon Tiegel, Bruce Bennett, Charles Maslin, and Phil at Tekserve.

CONTENTS

INTRODUCTION

Sometime in the late 1980s, a journalist complained in print that AC/DC had made ten albums that all sounded the same. When confronted with this accusation, Angus Young, the band's cofounder, lead guitarist and most visually identifiable member, was quick to respond.

"He's a liar," said Angus. "We've made eleven albums that all sound the same."

That statement goes a long way toward encapsulating AC/DC's appeal. Over the course of two decades, this tenacious quintet—helmed by Angus and his older brother, rhythm guitarist Malcolm Young—has carved out a singular niche in the rock world, thanks largely to its stubborn refusal to alter the simple, aggressive and decidedly unsubtle musical style that's always been the group's stock-in-trade. In the process, AC/DC has emerged as one of the essential cornerstones of contemporary hard rock.

Over the course of two decades and sixteen albums, AC/DC has consistently stuck to its guns, thrashing out earthy, good-humored anthems of debauchery and damnation while ignoring transient musical trends and social movements. As disdainful of preening prefab hard-rockers as they are of self-consciously serious artistes, these decidedly working-class dark horses have survived and prevailed through all manner of personal and professional struggles. With a refreshing absence of pretense, sophistication or intellectual analysis, they've never allowed such minor irritants as critical revilement, the passage of time or even death to get in the way of their go-for-the-throat mission.

Rising from the depths of Australia's rough-and-tumble club circuit to their current status as one of rock's most durable and respected arena attractions, AC/DC has always complemented its pummeling, no-frills sound with a distinctive visual identity built around the hyperactive stage antics of diminutive axe maniac Angus, whose trademark schoolboy uniform and faux-epileptic gyrations contrast with his offstage identity as a teetotaler who paints landscapes in his spare time. The four-fisted guitar attack of Angus and Malcolm was matched by the seething intensity of original frontman Bon Scott, whose image as a screaming hellion was all too reflective of his hell-raising, hard-drinking lifestyle.

After Scott's alcohol-induced accidental death—which came at a time when AC/DC was perched on the brink of worldwide superstardom—the ever-resilient band quickly regrouped with new singer Brian Johnson, whose raspy vocal style and salt-of-the-earth stage presence quickly became a key component of the band's collective persona. Despite a couple of subsequent changes in the group's drum seat, AC/DC's long-standing core of the Young brothers, Johnson and bassist Cliff Williams has remained intact as one of rock's most reliable—and incorrigible—institutions.

Despite its consistent popularity, in many respects AC/DC has never really fit in. Thanks to their songs' rowdy, risqué subject matter and the eardrum-shattering volume level of their live shows, they're commonly classified as a heavy-metal band. But AC/DC's self-effacing sense of humor and pared-down musical values have always kept it from slotting comfortably into the metal genre. Indeed, the group has always maintained a gritty rawness that underlines a deeply rooted spiritual connection to the blues and early rock 'n' roll that originally inspired the Young brothers—something that most bands in the hard-rock genre can't claim.

In an industry in which bands come and go with alarming frequency, AC/DC has maintained a remarkable longevity, remaining a going concern for over two decades without ever stooping to writing a ballad or a sincere sociopolitical anthem. With a deeply felt understanding of the power of a bone-crunching riff and a well-directed power chord, AC/DC has steadfastly refused to compromise the purity of its vision or make concessions to trendiness or artistic pretension. AC/DC remains blissfully unconcerned with fashion—and thus immune to the whims of the marketplace. Because they've never tried to be fashionable, they've never had to worry about going out of fashion.

AC/DC has emerged from its travails with its integrity and identity fully intact, confirming the band's identity as a group of unpretentious, down-to-earth guys who treat their fans with consideration and respect, while maintaining a healthy skepticism toward the standard trappings of rock stardom. While consistently inspiring fierce loyalty among their fans, they've gradually earned the grudging respect of the same critics who'd initially ridiculed the band's single-minded musical agenda.

In recent years, various self-appointed guardians of public decency have attempted to link AC/DC's music to all manner of depravities, from satanism to sexual perversion to serial murder. But anyone even passingly familiar with this relentlessly earthy band's repertoire knows that AC/DC isn't invoking anything more sinister than a rowdy, raucous good time. Though they're rude and bawdy enough to annoy your parents, there's never been anything cruel or mean-spirited about these veteran hellraisers.

AC/DC has always prided itself on its straightforwardness and lack of pretense. But if the music is proudly and defiantly basic, the band's story is a bit more complex . . .

1

WHO MADE WHO

Glasgow, Scotland, in the early 1960s was a rough, crowded industrial town whose depressed economy offered few options for working-class families. At the same time that much of Britain was experiencing economic hard times, a postwar boom was still in force in Australia. That underpopulated continent, bursting with natural resources but lacking sufficient population to fully exploit them, was particularly eager to encourage struggling Brits to emigrate to its shores.

In 1947 Australia had instituted a massive immigration program. Despite a significant influx of economically beleaguered Britons yearning for the challenge of a new frontier, newcomers arrived in numbers that fell short of the government's expectations. The Australian government subsequently instituted the Assisted Passage Scheme, which allowed immigrants to sail southward for a mere ten pounds (about twenty-five dollars at the time) a head. Many working-class Scottish families answered the call.

One such family was that of William and Margaret Young, who emigrated to Australia in 1963. As Angus, the last born of the Youngs' eight children, later told the British music weekly *Sounds,* "Me dad couldn't get work in Scotland. He found it impossible to support a family of our size, so he decided to try his luck down under."

Malcolm Young was born on January 6, 1953, in Glasgow. His brother Angus came into the world on March 31, 1955 (although some accounts would later push the date of Angus's birth back by one to four years). Malcolm and Angus were the youngest of eight children, the next in line being George, whose own musical experiences would soon make him a crucial influence on Malcolm and Angus. Just above George in the Young pecking order was brother Alex, who'd become a professional musician before the rest of his family left Scotland, playing in the Big Six, which succeeded the pre-stardom Beatles as Hamburg-based English rocker Tony Sheridan's backing group. In the late sixties, Alex would record for the Beatles' Apple label as a member of the avant-garde combo Grapefruit.

But Angus and Malcolm's introduction to rock 'n' roll came through their eldest sibling and only sister, also named Margaret, who while growing up in Glasgow had become a devotee of the raw early rock 'n' roll sounds of such American artists as Chuck Berry, Little Richard and Fats Domino, whose U.S. releases found their way into town through the city's seaport. Margaret's listening habits introduced Angus and Malcolm to the gritty, elemental power of black Ameri-

---

Portrait of the artist as a young axe maniac.
(Dick Barnatt, Redferns/Retna)

can music. It was one of the most important lessons they'd ever learn.

"When I was six or seven, [Margaret] took me to see Louis Armstrong," Angus later recalled. "I liked the way he smiled, the big teeth. Some people, you get goose bumps when they perform, and he was one. You could tell he was honest, a good man and a happy man."

Thanks to the influx of recent immigrants, Australia's national character in the first half of the 1960s was rather schizophrenic, divided between the traditional ties of its British immigrant population and a more modern obsession with the bigger-than-life symbols of American pop culture. This cultural schism was reflected in the decidedly shaky early stirrings of Australian rock 'n' roll.

Like many aspects of down-under culture, Australia's version of rock music started off several steps behind its American cousin. In America the rock 'n' roll explosion had been brewing in the steady erosion of social conventions that had begun around the end of World War II. In geographically and culturally isolated Australia, teenagers, for the most part, had yet to rebel against their parents, and kids and adults still pretty much listened to the same music. While Britain would outgrow its own awkward early attempts at mimicking American rock 'n' roll and begin carving out a rock 'n' roll tradition of its own in the early 1960s, Australia—where U.S. R&B discs were rarely released, denying young listeners access to the raw material that inspired the explosion of white American rock 'n' roll—would have to wait several more years to produce a credible homegrown rock act. Indeed, the most prominent of Australia's early rockers, Johnny O'Keefe, was but a pallid imitation of his American predecessors.

While the three eldest Young boys, like their father, settled into factory jobs, it didn't take George Young long to discover his true calling. Shortly after the Young family settled in the Sydney suburb of Burwood—an immigrant enclave that played host to a thriving garage-band scene—the budding guitarist/songwriter put a band together with a quartet of fellow transplants, Brits Stevie Wright (vocals) and Snowy Fleet (drums) and Dutchmen Harry Vanda (guitar) and Dick Diamond (bass). It's ironically appropriate that the Easybeats, which would soon prove to be Australia's first truly significant rock band, was comprised entirely of non-Australians.

The Easybeats began playing in late 1964 and quickly distinguished themselves from the local competition. Savvy, sharply dressed and sexier than other Australian combos, with a riveting frontman in Wright, the fivesome possessed a genuine performing and songwriting flair that marked them as the first Australian group to possess the talent, charisma and vision to potentially break into the international pop scene.

Through their manager, Mike Vaughan, the Easybeats met Ted Albert, a twenty-something music-publishing mogul who represented the third generation of Australia's oldest and most respected music-publishing house, J. Albert and Son, which had been established in the 1880s. The company would eventually emerge as a key force in the Australian rock scene and play a major role in the career of AC/DC, but in the mid-1960s it was just getting its feet wet in the pop market. Convinced that Australia was on the verge of a homegrown popular-music revolution in which the Easybeats could play a significant role, Ted formed Albert Productions, a production company offshoot of J. Albert and Son, and launched the new venture by signing the Easybeats.

Albert's gamble quickly paid off. In the summer of 1965 the Easybeats became major Australian stars with their second single, "She's So Fine," which began a run of hits. "Easyfever," an Antipodean answer to Beatlemania, was soon a national phenomenon. One day Angus Young returned home from school to find that hundreds of young girls had descended upon his family's house, hoping to get a look at his pop-star brother. As Angus later recalled, "One day George was a sixteen-year-old sitting on his bed playing guitar, the next day he was worshipped by the whole country."

While the scene undoubtedly planted some awareness of stardom's fringe benefits in the young Angus's mind, a more immediate concern at the time was the fact that the local police had set up barricades around the house and wouldn't let Angus through.

The Easybeats did manage to achieve some degree of success overseas. The band's biggest hit was the anthemic 1967 single "Friday on My Mind," which rose to number 6 in Britain and number 16 in the U.S. and has remained a rock standard, thanks to its perfect encapsulation of the frustrations of nine-to-five life and the emotional release provided by the weekend. By the time that song was released, the Easybeats had relocated to London. But while the band scored a few more minor international hits and remained major stars in Australia, a combination of managerial inexperience and loss of musical focus kept them from further expanding their audience, and in 1970 the Easybeats disbanded.

2

PROBLEM CHILD

One cannot understate the influence of the Easybeats on both Australian musical history and Angus and Malcolm Young. As the brothers grew increasingly frustrated with the staid, conservative society in which they were growing up, they turned to rock 'n' roll as an outlet for their frustrations.

"In my family," Angus recalled, "music was always there, probably because there were a lot of brothers that were playing music from different generations. Music was never looked at as a bad thing, it was always looked at as a good thing . . . There was always a record player around or always a radio on. And I never heard my father say, 'You can't listen to that.' They always felt, the more music the better."

But Angus and Malcolm were not encouraged by their parents to follow Alex and George's lead in pursuing music as a career choice. For Angus, the Easybeats were "definitely an inspiration," but "Mal and me were kept away from them. In school, you got frowned upon because obviously your brother or your family was an influence to rebel. At that time, it was better for us not to be sort of pushed at it. My parents thought we'd be better off doing something else."

So it was that Mr. and Mrs. Young were probably less than pleased when their two youngest children revealed their plans to pursue careers as rock musicians. "We didn't get much encouragement," stated Malcolm, adding, "Dad was still asking George when he was going to get a proper job."

As it happened, Angus's and Malcolm's academic careers didn't bode well for their chances in more conventional fields of endeavor. Malcolm, upon arriving in Australia, had wasted little time in earning a reputation as a schoolyard brawler. Angus, despite showing a talent for art, was an unenthusiastic student—and the frequent recipient of corporal punishment, which was still common in Australian schools. "I was caned the first day," said Angus. "The guy said, 'What's your name?' 'Young.' 'Come out here, I'm going to make an example of you.'

"I was an unhappy schoolboy," Angus confessed. "Always played truant. I was a bad pupil and only really liked art because you could do what you liked. I once made a six-foot-long fly out of papier-mâché which scared the shit out of everyone on the bus home.

"It was so military," Angus recalled of his educational background. "They seemed to take great pride in keeping you in the dark. They didn't seem to want you to know what was going on in the rest of the world. I was really surprised at the way people lived outside Australia when I left it. People were getting away with a lot more than I ever did."

When the Easybeats hit it big, Angus's headmaster vented his anti–rock 'n' roll sentiment by ordering him to cut his hair and telling him that his big brother had entered "a profession for perverts." This brought out the feistier side of Mrs. Young, who informed the educator that Angus's family would be the ones to decide when he would have his hair cut. "She didn't like us being bullied about by authority," Angus said.

"I wasn't really a bad sort of kid," insisted Angus. "I mean, I listened. If I wanted to learn something, my old man used to say, 'Angus, do yourself a favor. There's a library down the road, go in there.' When I'd truant, that was the first place I'd head to. It was great. There'd be racks of the magazine *Down Beat* from America which had articles on Muddy Waters. And I liked reading about that. So I much preferred going there because they didn't sell it at the newsstands."

As is common for working-class Australian kids, Angus was given the choice of leaving school just before reaching the age of fifteen. He opted to cash in his chips after being presented with what he would later describe as "a very fine option—'Either you leave or we'll throw you out.' If you weren't there for so many days a year, they figured you weren't worth teaching, so they got rid of you."

As Angus recalled, "At fourteen and nine months—that was the legal age you could leave school—the headmaster lined us all up and said, 'Well, morning guys, you're at that age. You know, the leaving age.' He sort of said, 'Well, Mr. Young, you're lazy. You're never here, so . . .' "

In Australia at the time, according to Angus, "There were not many choices out there, really, when you come from a sort of a working-class background. The options for me and Malcolm both were the factory."

Actually, Angus put in stints as a janitor and typesetter, while Malcolm worked as sewing-machine maintenance mechanic in a brassiere factory. While toiling at their unfulfilling jobs during the day, both Angus and Malcolm whiled away their evenings playing with a variety of local bands.

In 1971 the eighteen-year-old Malcolm had joined the rather oddly named Velvet Underground. Not to be confused with Lou Reed and John Cale's groundbreaking New York–based band of the same name, these Velvets had formed in New-castle, England, in 1967 but had recently relocated to the Syd-ney area and specialized in covers of songs by American West Coast bands like the Doors and Jefferson Airplane. With Mal-colm (who insisted on adding several numbers by his then idol, Marc Bolan, to the set) and Australian vocalist Andy Imlah added to the lineup, the Velvet Underground became a pop-ular attraction on Sydney's dance-club circuit. The gig allowed Malcolm to quit his job and begin earning a living from play-ing music.

A frequent onlooker at Malcolm's gigs was Angus, who would stand directly in front of the stage and stare awestruck at his brother. At the time, Angus—then sporting a skinhead haircut—was already wielding his trademark Gibson SG, jam-ming informally with friends and playing at home for Malcolm and his bandmates. Even then, Angus, who had received a few formal guitar lessons at age eleven but was for the most part a self-taught musician, wouldn't play any chords, just leads. "I jumped ahead when I was first starting out," he admits. "I learned a solo before I learned a chord."

Whatever Angus may have lacked in subtlety, he made up in style. "I was always small, and I'd go to those clubs right after school," he later told *Hit Parader*. "Most of the guys who were hanging out there were much older and really tough looking. For some reason they just took to me. They'd let me play with their bands, and once they found out that people were actually coming to see me play, they started advertising the fact that I was with their band."

The older musicians would often bill Angus as "the baby guitar star"—an appropriate enough nickname, since Angus was underage at the time. "The club owners used to say, 'How old is the little guy?' And we'd always have to lie and say, 'Oh, he's a dwarf.' That got me in."

Even then, Angus knew that this was what he wanted to do with his life. "*I* had drive. I wanted to do it and I knew I'd do it. I just wanted people to sit up and take notice of me . . . I never mellowed. I never changed. I just stuck at it."

Following the Easybeats' breakup, George Young and Harry Vanda returned to Australia to work as a songwriting/production team for Albert Productions. The pair would eventually help define a vital strain of raucous Australian hard rock, working with AC/DC and other Australian acts like the Angels (aka Angel City) and Rose Tattoo.

At the time, though, George and Harry were working on an album of their own, *Tales of Old Granddaddy,* under the nom de disc guise of the Marcus Hook Roll Band. The project had begun in London as a casual, tongue-in-cheek diversion but took on a more serious aura after EMI's American division expressed interest in a full album by the pseudonymous outfit. In the process, Vanda and Young recruited George's younger brothers as supporting players.

"That was the first thing that Malcolm and Angus did before AC/DC," George later told Australian rock journalist Glenn A. Baker. "We didn't take it very seriously, so we thought we'd include them to give them an idea of what recording was all about."

By the end of 1972 Malcolm was working steadily with the Velvet Underground, often doing double duty at gigs by playing their own sets and backing up singer Ted Mulry, a member of the Albert Productions stable. But Malcolm was growing increasingly impatient with the Velvet Underground's unimaginative repertoire and was eager to be involved with music a bit closer to his own heart. So he quit, determined to start a new band that would be a more accurate representation of his own musical desires.

The Marcus Hook Roll Band project had had a profound effect on Malcolm Young, who decided that the standard process of overdubbing tracks one by one went against his idea of how rock 'n' roll ought to be made. He decided that *his* band wouldn't do that. Indeed, Malcolm had some very specific ideas about the kind of band he wanted to be a member of.

3

IT'S A LONG WAY TO THE TOP
(IF YOU WANNA ROCK 'N' ROLL)

While his older brother was hatching plans for his dream band, Angus was well on his way toward establishing a distinctive stage persona. He later told *Rip* magazine that his spasmodic, seemingly out-of-control onstage body language has always come naturally. "For some unknown reason, whenever I'm playing, it's like, being a little guy, where most people bend a note on a guitar, my whole body bends. Then when I hit a chord down at the bottom end of the guitar, I just follow it. Other guys let their fingers do the walking. With me, the body does the walking."

Such trademark Angus moves as his patented duckwalk and his on-the-floor body spasms could be handy attention-getting devices when playing for drunken, rowdy barroom crowds. Many of these gestures grew out of accidents. One night, Angus remembers, the pre-AC/DC combo he was playing with was "going down really badly. I walked across the stage and tripped over the guitar lead, so I felt a right dick, y'know, and I kept rolling across the floor. I made it look like a big death scene, screaming all hell from the guitar. It was the only clap we got all night. Told Malcolm about it, and he said he was formin' a new band. He said, 'Come and do that with me band.' "

Though Angus may not have had a clear picture of what he wanted to do with his life, he had a pretty good idea of what he *didn't* want to do. "I was not going to work," he told *Circus*. "I was pretty determined on that fact. I remember my father saying 'You and Malcolm playing together, you'll last a week,' 'cause we used to fight like cat and dog."

Malcolm had initially intended to be the only guitarist in his as-yet-unnamed new combo but had a last-minute change of heart and decided to add Angus—instead of a piano player— to the lineup. Joining Malcolm and Angus in AC/DC's original incarnation were vocalist Dave Evans, Dutch-born bassist Larry Van Knedt and drummer Colin Burgess, who had previously pounded the skins with the popular Adelaide band, the Masters Apprentices.

Frontman Evans, a Newcastle native whom Malcolm had met during his Velvet Underground years and whom Angus would later dismiss as "a bit of a Gary Glitter freak," was a flamboyant, stack-heeled glamster whose hammy stage antics contrasted the down-to-earth image that AC/DC would later project. Though he wasn't much of a singer, Evans's image of outrageousness was in keeping with the glitter-rock direction that Malcolm favored at the time.

As Angus explained, "When we started, we didn't care about getting on the radio and we didn't care what people said about us. We just knew what we felt was missing from music at the time. We just went out and played rock music."

The quintet's first public appearance took place in a small

Sydney club called Chequers on New Year's Eve, welcoming in 1974 with a set comprised largely of covers of songs by the likes of The Beatles, The Rolling Stones and Chuck Berry. Though the band had yet to find its true sound, witnesses agree that, even at this embryonic stage, their musical fire-power was quite impressive. "We had been together for about two weeks," Angus later recalled. "We had to get up and blast away. From the word go it went great. Everyone thought we were a pack of loonies . . . you know, 'Who's been feeding them kids bananas?' "

By this point, Angus was already wearing his trademark school uniform on stage. "I started wearing my schoolboy suit," he explained, "because the first band I was in rehearsed right after school, so I was already wearing it. The next group I was in liked the way I looked in the suit . . . It got them a lot of attention, and by the time AC/DC started, a lot of people expected to see me wearing my schoolboy suit."

On other occasions though, Angus has claimed that the costume grew out of more practical considerations. "I used to wear shorts because they were easier to get around in than jeans. When you'd sweat a lot, they'd cling and stick to your legs. So I figured I'd take a hint off footballers and wear a pair of shorts. From that, me sister came up with the idea, 'Why don't you just put your school suit on?' You see, I was going to school in Sydney at the time, and I had me school blazer, 'cause kids there wear uniforms. So I got an old cap, put a big 'A' on it, and there it was!

"When I first put on the schoolboy suit, I thought, 'Well, you must look crazy in this school suit and everything, so you've got to show something else. You can't just walk on and expect everything to happen.' So I just kept adding to the act, and it got more and more outrageous. But I always had that walk and hopping thing. I just can't play if I've got to stand still. And ever since I can remember, I've always moved me 'ead when I heard music."

Whatever its origins, Angus's demented stage persona added a surreal sense of showmanship to the early AC/DC's relatively straightforward presentation, offering a potent if somewhat bizarre symbol of the band's implicit social rebellion. In the early days, though, the diminutive axe hero's look could confuse club audiences.

"It was like a cold slap in the face," Angus stated. "They thought, 'Is this a joke?' . . . People would sort of giggle. And Malcolm would say to me, 'Shut 'em up! You can play!' It was a good thing, because they were going to remember us for the little guy in the short pants who looks like he's having an epileptic fit."

According to some accounts, it was sister Margaret who suggested the name AC/DC, after noticing it amid the electrical information on her sewing machine. Angus has also claimed that he first spotted the phrase on his mom's vacuum cleaner. The Young brothers have always adamantly maintained that the name was a reference to electrical current rather than sexual orientation, claiming to have been unaware that the term was slang for bisexuality.

Though the band would continue to vigorously deny any sexual connotations suggested by their name, in a 1974 interview with the Australian rock magazine *Go-Set,* Malcolm allowed that "if people want to think we're five camp guys, then that's okay with us." Indeed, confusion over the name became so rampant that the band was often booked to play at gay-themed events, and the gig-hungry band wasn't about to turn down the work.

By April 1974 AC/DC's original rhythm section had been supplanted by bassist Rob Bailey and drummer Peter Clack. It was this lineup that would record AC/DC's debut single,

Angus and Malcolm's composition "Can I Sit Next to You Girl," with George Young and Harry Vanda producing. Though a rather unremarkable debut, the song nonetheless became a minor regional hit in Perth and Adelaide.

Malcolm, meanwhile, was brought in by George to contribute some guitar work to *Hard Road,* the LP that he and Harry were producing for ex-Easybeats singer Stevie Wright, who since that group's breakup had fallen into both heroin addiction and the Sydney cast of the stage musical *Jesus Christ Superstar. Hard Road* yielded a major Australian hit in "Evie," and AC/DC was given a choice spot opening a free show at the Sydney Opera House, which also featured a headlining set in which Wright backed by a pickup band that included Malcolm as well as George and Harry.

AC/DC's opening set prompted *Go-Set* to proclaim that the band "showed they're a force to be reckoned with. They play rock 'n' roll intelligently, adding their own ideas to sure crowd-pleasers like 'Heartbreak Hotel,' 'No Particular Place to Go' and 'Shake, Rattle and Roll.' " The review further noted that the band "looked great and sounded great. Their material is part original and will undoubtedly prove popular as the band gets about a little more."

George Young would continue to be a key player in AC/DC's early success, not only through his production skills but also through the hard-won experience he'd gained during his Easybeats days. Mindful of the career setbacks that his own band had suffered as a result of naiveté and inexperience, George passed on much useful wisdom that was invaluable in helping AC/DC to avoid repeating many of his mistakes. Not the least of these was the importance of staying in touch with their rock 'n' roll roots, which the Easybeats had failed to do once they began to experiment with more eclectic styles.

Though in later years Angus and Malcolm would paint

AC/DC's early days as a rise from utter obscurity—and there is obviously a fair amount of truth in that contention—it should also be noted that the band did have the benefit of the financial resources of the Albert empire as well as the connections and career guidance of George Young and Harry Vanda. George, in particular, was also indispensable in helping to construct AC/DC's trademark sound, focusing the band's raw power without attempting to polish it for mass consumption.

"It was incredible how fast things happened for us," marveled Angus. "George knew who to contact at recording studios and radio stations, and that made things a lot easier for us."

Whatever help they had in the studio and in the business realm, once the band got onstage, they were on their own. "We were one of the only Australian bands that was playing original songs," Angus points out. "The others were playing Zeppelin or Deep Purple songs in bars, but we had our sights set on a bigger goal.

"[The] clubs could be a little rough-and-tumble," said Angus. "Many a guy dived onstage. One clown, once in Perth, the guy's at me all night, gets onstage and puts me in a headlock. That was it then. So I defended myself. Well, he got in for the shock of his life. I know I look teeny up there, but that's the worst time to give me grief. When I put that school suit on, I go into another thing. It takes over. Malcolm says, 'It's like he's possessed!' It is two different people. And this clown decides he's going to come into your planet. You know, I decided to evict him."

The gnarliest snarl in rock,
in action at the 1976 Reading Festival.
[Erica Echenberg, Rederns/Retna]

Despite the more trying aspects of AC/DC's early club gigs, the experience proved invaluable in teaching the group the finer points of winning over an indifferent crowd. One example cited by Angus: "One night playing a pub in Australia, we were going down like a lead weight. You could almost feel the audience thinking, 'Is that all they can do?' So I lost my cool— well, if they don't like it, I'm going to have some fun. So I went out and played all around the tables and danced on top of the tables. Another night, I ended up with just two strings left on my guitar. Malcolm said, 'Yeah, but what a guitar solo you gave with those two strings, Angus!' I was playing for a good half hour with two strings."

That summer, with George's approval, AC/DC hired its first manager, Dennis Laughlin, another transplanted Scotsman who had grown up near Burwood and who had sung with the popular Australian pop-rock band Sherbet. One of Laughlin's first orders of business was to get AC/DC on the road, in order to exploit the live circuit that lay beyond Sydney. To that end, Laughlin managed to land the group a high-profile slot as the support act on Lou Reed's August tour of Australia.

By this point, Angus and Malcolm had decided that AC/DC was in desperate need of a new frontman, as the vocal deficiencies and flamboyant stage shtick of leather-studded Dave Evans were increasingly at odds with the straight-ahead attitude favored by Angus and Malcolm. "We used to kick him offstage," Angus later said of Evans, "and me and Malcolm would just jam on boogies and old Chuck Berry songs, and the band would go down better without him."

4

BAD BOY BOOGIE

Bon Scott spent the first six years of his life in the small town of Kirriemuir, located—prophetically enough—in the county of Angus in southeast Scotland. Kirriemuir is best known as the birthplace of *Peter Pan* author J. M. Barrie and in the eighteenth century was the home of a thriving trade in jute, a fiber used in the manufacture of canvas. By the time Ronald Belford Scott was born on July 9, 1946, however, Kirriemuir was in the throes of economic depression.

Bon's father, Charles, known to friends and relations as Chick, had worked in the local family bakery business in Kirriemuir before serving in the British Army in World War II. During the war, he met Isobelle Cunningham, more familiarly known as Isa, in Kirkcaldy, a port city near Edinburgh; the two were married in 1941 and settled in Kirriemuir after Chick received his discharge at the end of 1945. Both Chick and Isa hailed from musical families, and music was an integral part of their married life as well; Chick played drums in the Kirriemuir Pipe Band and performed with the local light-opera company.

In 1952, when Bon was six, the Scott family—which by then included another son, Derek, and would be joined the following year by another, Graeme—relocated to Australia, where Isa's sister had moved the year before. The Scotts first resided in Melbourne before settling in the Adelaide suburb of Sunshine. In 1956 Graeme was diagnosed with asthma, and the Scott family relocated to the drier climate of Fremantle, a quiet port town just south of Perth.

While the young Bon (or Ron, as his parents still refer to him) demonstrated a rebellious streak from an early age, he also had a healthy relationship with his parents. From them, he learned the politeness and personality that would regularly help to get him out of scrapes in his later life. As early as grade school, Bon had shown an affinity for music, first playing recorder in school; he would subsequently have brief flirtations with piano and accordion, before settling on drums.

Bon took his first tentative steps as a performer at the age of twelve, playing a recorder duet with a classmate at a school concert and banging the drums alongside his dad in the local Caledonian Society's Scots pipe band. His progress with the latter group earned Bon the status of novice champion, not to mention an appearance on local TV. But this was the late fifties, and the first faint echoes of American rock 'n' roll were beginning to reach Australia. It wouldn't take long for the red-haired young rapscallion to answer the call of the wild.

While becoming increasingly proficient as a drummer, Bon found other outlets for his boundless energy, like honing his high-diving skills and sharpening his reputation as a proficient street fighter whose scrappiness belied his small size. Like music, those activities gained him an exhilarating sense of freedom. Perhaps more important, they also won him attention from the opposite sex. Though he performed well enough in school, Bon's lifelong distaste for authority led him to quit his studies as soon as he was legally able, at the age of fifteen.

After leaving school, he held a series of odd jobs, driving a tractor, laboring on fishing boats and working as an apprentice weighing-machine mechanic. When he wasn't working, Bon was busy cultivating the style of a leather-jacketed, slick-haired rocker, a look that echoed his musical tastes, which ran to the work of uninhibited American performers like Elvis Presley, Jerry Lee Lewis, Little Richard and Chuck Berry, who were among the few genuine rockers Australian kids were able to hear at the time. It was during this period that Bon got the first of his trademark tattoos, an elaborate vinelike display just above his waist. The painful swelling that came along with the tattoo assured that it would be weeks before he could close his jeans again.

A local band called the Nomads regularly staged dances at Perth's Port Beach, where the teenage Bon would often get up to warble a rock 'n' roll number with the group. At one of these dances, Bon, after fighting off a group of boys attempting to shanghai his date, fled from the police by car, only to be nabbed after trying to steal some gasoline. He was arrested and, according to a news report printed in the *West Australian,* "pleaded guilty to charges of having given a false name and address to the police, having escaped legal custody, having unlawful carnal knowledge and having stolen twelve gallons of petrol." As a youthful offender, the sixteen-year-old Bon was left in the custody of the Child Welfare Department and was remanded to the Riverbank boys' home.

According to Clinton Walker's Scott biography, *Highway to Hell,* the court had actually given Bon the option of being released into his parents' custody, but he was so ashamed of his brush with the law that he chose to do time rather than face his mother and father. Indeed, he was so guilt-stricken by the thought of having let Chick and Isa down that he refused to see them when they attempted to visit. If the bleak nine-month stretch that Bon had served in the military discipline of Riverbank in some ways strengthened his nonconformism, it also helped sway him from his delinquent ways.

It was during his time in Riverbank that Bon had begun thinking about pursuing music as a career option. During recreation periods, he'd play drums in a combo he'd formed with two other inmates, and his enjoyment of the resulting racket convinced him that he wanted to carve out a livelihood as a drummer. Upon returning to the outside world, he set up his drum kit in his parents' living room and began thinking about how he could get into a band.

Fortunately, Bon had picked a good time to take an active interest in rock 'n' roll, since the rising Australian popularity of the Beatles and the Rolling Stones had inspired a small beat-group scene to spring up in the Perth area. With three friends, Bon formed his first band, the Spektors, in early 1965, gracing audiences at local youth clubs with renditions of Beatles and Stones tunes along with a sprinkling of garage-band standards like Them's "Gloria." Though singer John Collins was the Spektors' official frontman, Bon would periodically step up to the mike to take over vocals while Collins manned the drums. Those occasional vocal spots brought out Bon's natural charisma and showmanship and suggested to him that his future might lie in singing rather than drumming.

Within a year, the Spektors (who practiced at the Scott home) was one of the area's most popular local bands. But stardom in Perth was a somewhat limited distinction, and it was obvious that more musical firepower would be required if the band was going to grow into something more than a weekend diversion. As it happened, another local semipro outfit, the Winztons, was thinking along similar lines, so the two combos joined forces to form a more self-consciously goal-oriented group, the Valentines.

Vince Lovegrove, the Winztons' leader and frontman, would later recall in the pages of the Australian music paper *RAM*, "Bon was the cute little drummer with cute little eyes, pixie-like ears, a cute turned-up nose, a cute little Scottish accent, and about four very obvious tattoos. In rock 'n' roll in those days, you could go a long way being cute."

As it happened, cuteness would not prove to be the key to Bon Scott's success.

5

SHOW BUSINESS

Upon joining the more ambitious, professional Valentines, Bon traded in his drum kit for a vocal mike. He shared lead-vocal duties with Vince Lovegrove, whose savvy and experience established him as the band's natural leader—and a friendly rival to Bon, who couldn't be bothered with business details. The Valentines performed in snappy matching blue suits and augmented their stage act with flash bombs and other visual frills. The band's repertoire consisted largely of covers of American soul hits and songs by such popular British acts as the Who and the Small Faces; much of the material was drawn from the record library of the group's manager, Allan Robertson, a DJ at Perth radio station 6KY.

Having automatically inherited all of the Spektors' and the Winztons' bookings, the Valentines quickly consolidated their preeminent position on the Perth scene. But the band's attempts to carve out an identity as a recording act were less than auspicious. In May 1967 they released a debut single on the small independent label Clarion, but the derivative disc was indicative of the lack of originality that would ultimately keep the Valentines from achieving musical distinction. The A-side was a rendition of American R&B singer Arthur Alexander's much-covered hit "Every Day I Have to Cry," and the flip was an obscure Small Faces tune, "Can't Dance With You." Despite its lack of originality, though, the single made it to the local Top 5, not a bad showing for a debut effort.

The Valentines scored a coup when they opened a pair of shows for the Easybeats at Her Majesty's Theater in Sydney. The event marked Bon's first encounter with George Young and Harry Vanda, who would eventually play a prominent role in his musical career. At the time, though, Bon was a lot more interested in the Easybeats' frontman, Stevie Wright, after whom Bon had initially patterned much of his performing persona.

The two bands hit it off so well that Vanda and Young wrote a song, "She Said," for the Valentines while the musicians partied after the shows. It was the first of three songs that the Easybeats would bequeath to the Valentines and would appear as the A-side of the band's second single. But even the Easybeats' most fervent admirers would have to admit that "She Said" was not one of their most engaging compositions. It didn't help that the Valentines backed it with an unrepentantly wimpy rendition of the Phil Spector pop chestnut "To Know Her Is to Love Her," which they retitled "To Know You Is to Love You." Understandably, this sophomore release bombed on the charts.

By that point, the Valentines had decided to move from Perth to the more cosmopolitan Melbourne, which in 1967 stood as Australia's rock capital. Such Melbourne-based acts as the Loved Ones, the Groop, Ronnie Burns, Normie Rowe and Bobby & Laurie, along with Adelaide transplants the Masters Apprentices and the Twilights (not to mention Bon's old Perth pal Johnny Young), would never really figure out how to process their influences into anything authentic or personal and would never really produce music of sufficient merit to cause any sleepless nights for their overseas contemporaries. But the Melbourne scene had an energy that made it clear that rock had become a permanent fixture on the Australian landscape.

Upon their arrival in Melbourne (which coincided with the release of "She Said"), the Valentines hooked up with a powerful management and booking agency, AMBO. Though they did manage to scrape up the occasional small-time tour, the band mainly played local (and usually sparsely attended) gigs. They lived hand-to-mouth in a house in the Melbourne suburb of Burwood—not far from the Young family home, where Angus and Malcolm were still struggling with puberty—and avoided starving only by shoplifting food from local supermarkets. Within this demoralizing state of affairs, it was generally the unflappable Bon who was responsible for keeping his bandmates' spirits from flagging.

The Valentines' third and fourth singles—"I Can Hear the Raindrops" and the psychedelipop Easybeats cover, "Peculiar Hole in the Sky," respectively—largely failed to catch the public's ear. But the group's efforts to establish itself on the live circuit were slowly but surely beginning to reap dividends.

By late 1968 the Australian charts had taken a turn toward more blatantly commercial sounds. It was in this atmosphere that the Valentines boldly announced, in an interview with Go-Set, that they were indeed a bubblegum group. The once-scruffy combo now sported a newly manicured image, including matching frilly shirts, flared trousers and beads; Bon even covered up his tattoos with makeup. In the same issue of

Go-Set, the singer filled out a profile in which he claimed to be nineteen (he was twenty-two) and listed his musical favorites as the Beatles, the Moody Blues, John Lee Hooker, Otis Redding, the Supremes and "Scottish Pipe Band music."

Meanwhile, the band's record company, Philips, inaugurated a media blitz to establish the newly made-over combo; during the holiday season, Australian media outlets received a Christmas card bearing the legend "The slogan for this year is 'Be my Valentine in '69.' " The campaign set the stage for the next Valentines single, which featured another Vanda/Young-penned A-side, "My Old Man's a Groovy Old Man," backed by a Pretty Things number, "Ebeneezer." Released, cleverly enough, on Valentine's Day 1969, the disc was a chart success, finally establishing the Valentines as genuine, teen-mayhem-inducing pop idols. On March 10, after the group played a free show for a seven-thousand-strong crowd at Alexandra Gardens during Melbourne's annual Moomba festival, a "riot" ensued in which Vince was arrested for assaulting a police officer after pushing an overeager cop from the stage with his bare foot.

Though the Valentines' new media image was clean and sweet, the members' lifestyle was considerably less so. In fact, the teen pinups had developed quite a reputation for their rampant carousing, dope-smoking and womanizing. Not surprisingly, the group quickly grew tired of its sanitized image. With a bit of commercial success under their belt—and with the Australian rock scene moving belatedly toward more progressive, self-consciously arty sounds—it wasn't long before the Valentines began feeling the need to make more "serious" music.

But this ambition was not reflected in the band's next single, "Nick Nack Paddy Whack," whose unabashedly cutesy nursery-rhyme rewrite did little for the band's artistic credibility. The song's B-side, "Getting Better"—which boasted Bon's first-ever songwriting credit, which he shared with bandmate Wyn Milson—at least possessed some historical significance, if not musical merit.

Even as they strove to gain credibility with "serious" rock fans, the Valentines managed to hold on to much of their young female following. In fact, the band's busy performing schedule often found them doing multiple gigs in the same night. After playing their more mainstream tunes at a couple of teen dances in local town halls, they'd end the night at a rock club, where they'd change from their matching suits into jeans and play their looser, more rocking material. It was at the latter events that Bon could really let loose and allow his natural performing abilities to shine through.

On September 20, 1969, police—reportedly acting on a tip from a member of another band who spilled the beans in order to save his own skin—raided the Valentines' practice space and found a quantity of marijuana. In the wake of the bust (and before the matter had come to trial), the band—rather recklessly—spoke out publicly in favor of the legalization of pot and against police harassment. In the closest he ever came to making a topical statement, the usually apolitical Bon said in one interview that the police "shouldn't persecute whole groups of people just for being different." In another, he stated, "The Australian government deserves a few ripples. They'll be the last to legalize homosexuality, and pot will be the same." In the wake of the bust, the band attempted to institute a self-imposed pot-smoking ban, which only served to heighten the internal tensions that were already threatening their future.

By the time the Valentines appeared in court in February to plead guilty on the pot charge (each escaped with a $150 fine), breakup rumors were already in the air. An April single release, the band-penned "Juliette," fell victim to Australian radio's temporary ban on major-label records, which had been instituted in response to the majors' attempts to extract payment from stations for the privilege of playing their releases. As a result, "Juliette" received little airplay and barely cracked the Top 30.

The chart failure of "Juliette" was enough to push the already shaky Valentines over the edge. The group officially called it quits on August 1, 1970. Bon Scott's days of being cute were officially over.

6

AIN'T NO FUN (WAITING AROUND TO BE A MILLIONAIRE)

Within six months of the Valentines' dissolution, Bon received a call from Bruce Howe, leader of a much-touted new band called Fraternity, inviting him to join his group. Fraternity had evolved from the Levi Smith Clefs, whose 1970 album *Empty Monkey* was something of a landmark at a time when full albums by Australian acts were still rare. In the post-Woodstock hippie-rock glow that had taken its sweet time in reaching Australia, Fraternity, somewhat unrealistically, viewed themselves as a sort of down-under answer to the Band.

By the time Bon—now sporting an elfin beard—joined Fraternity, the band had already recorded a single, "Why Did It Have to Be Me," and begun gigging around Adelaide, where it had relocated from its original base of Sydney. With a deal with the small Australian label Sweet Peach and some vague murmurings of interest from MCA in America, Fraternity had been the subject of much advance press hoopla, with Sydney's *Sunday Mirror* proclaiming them "rapidly on their way to becoming Australia's greatest hard-rock group."

But Fraternity's original promise fizzled out, thanks to a deadly combination of bad planning, bad attitude and disappointing music. Perhaps the band's fate was sealed when they decided to base themselves in Adelaide, far from the workings of the Australian music industry but near the base of manager Hamish Henry, a wealthy patron of the arts who'd taken the band under his wing and set the musicians up with housing, equipment and a regular salary.

While 1971 would prove to be something of a banner year for Australian rock, Fraternity would not benefit from the national scene's new vitality. The group's first single, recorded before (but released after) Bon's arrival, fared poorly in the charts. The album that the group eventually recorded, *Livestock* (on which Bon played some recorder as well as singing), went unreleased for over a year after its completion, and was both a musical and commercial disappointment, mixing compact, inventive rock tunes with artsily overwrought pieces.

Despite the disappointing album, which reputedly failed to capture the intensity of the band's live sets, Fraternity did manage a few career coups. They toured Australia supporting American rock 'n' roll legend Jerry Lee Lewis and performed at the Hamish Henry–financed Myponga festival, Adelaide's biggest rock event since the Beatles drew a crowd of 300,000 to a 1964 appearance there. But Fraternity's second single, "Seasons of Change," despite the presence of Bon's vocals, did little to enhance the band's prospects.

Living on a secluded farm in the hills seventeen miles outside of Adelaide, Fraternity attempted to emulate the much-mythologized lifestyle of their idols, the Band, whose communal existence in Woodstock, New York, had produced

Bon and Angus finding their stage legs.
[Dick Barnatt, Redferns/Retna]

the classic album *Music From Big Pink*. But with manager Henry footing the bills and no particular pressure to actually produce anything, the farm's near-constant party atmosphere didn't inspire much in the way of creativity. Indeed, the two albums that the band would record during its three-year existence included, between them, barely a dozen original compositions.

Though Fraternity liked to project an image of communal democracy, the group actually had a well-established pecking order in which Bon, despite being the frontman, possessed relatively little clout. He was rarely allowed to write lyrics for Fraternity songs; much of what he did write during his time with the band would eventually surface in AC/DC songs.

October 1971 saw the release of two Fraternity singles, "The Race," a *Livestock* outtake released by Sweet Peach, and the new, boogie-oriented "If You Got It," which the band released on its own Raven label. Though the latter fared well on the South Australian charts, Fraternity's second album, *Flaming Galah* (released on Raven through RCA), did little to encourage much faith in the band's future, containing only three new songs, along with several numbers reworked and rerecorded from the first album.

Despite Fraternity's general lack of productivity, the band's frequent Adelaide gigs established it as a local legend. Those gigs helped toughen Fraternity's sound, with the group's art-rock excesses giving way to a tougher, more immediate edge. Indeed, in live situations the band occasionally received flak for its excessive use of volume. One such instance occurred at a show in conservative Queensland, at which the cops insisted the band turn down the volume, and the street-smart but politically naive Bon responded with an onstage speech that gave the police all the excuse they needed to shut down the show.

Fraternity had initially discussed the possibility of touring America in 1972; instead, they decided to relocate to England, where Hamish Henry had some music-business contacts. In hindsight the decision to concentrate on Britain seems ill-advised. While a U.S. tour might have helped to reverse the band's sagging fortunes, Fraternity's brand of scruffy rural rock was completely out of fashion in Britain, which at the time was obsessed with the first wave of glam rock in the form of David Bowie, T. Rex and Mott the Hoople.

Though Henry set the band up with the high-powered MAM booking agency and a well-connected comanager, Tony MacArthur, the year and a half that Fraternity spent living in the London suburb of Finchley ultimately sapped the band's momentum and morale. Living under the same roof in relative poverty didn't help matters, further exacerbating the band members' personal differences. It also took a serious toll on Bon's relationship with his new wife, Irene, whom he'd wed just before the move to England in order to get Henry to pick up the tab for her airfare.

Despite having a powerful booking agency behind them, Fraternity's live work during their stay in England amounted to a handful of British gigs and a short tour of Germany. Eventually, the band members' wives had to go out and find jobs, while the musicians generally sat around waiting for success to fall into their laps. Bon was particularly frustrated by the infrequency of his opportunities to perform, to the point that he took the very uncharacteristic step of getting a day job of his own, working in a wig factory.

In a rather desperate attempt to invoke some connection with current English rock tastes, Fraternity eventually changed its name to Fang. In April 1973 Fang played a couple of shows with Geordie, a Slade-styled Newcastle combo fronted by gravel-throated screamer Brian Johnson. Years later, Bon would remark to his AC/DC bandmates how impressed he'd been by Johnson's singing.

In May, Fang played a short tour on which the group was mismatched with German art-rock ensemble Amon Duul. Just how quaint Fang's style must have seemed in that context was driven home by a review in the *Gloucestershire Echo,* which dismissed Fang as "unambitious but multi-decibel," adding that the band's songs "sounded much like the rhythm-and-blues material that was churned out by a million would-be Rolling Stones in the early '60s."

Meanwhile, as interband relations continued to sour, Bon's devil-may-care approach toward life and limb began to assert itself more frequently. The most obvious example, perhaps, was the death scare that occurred after he consumed a quantity of datura, a poisonous plant that supposedly possessed psychedelic properties.

In August, Fang played what would be its final show, at a small festival in Windsor. Soon after, Hamish Henry, whose hefty financial investment in the band was continuing to lose him money, even as the musicians he was supporting grew to blame him for their ongoing lack of success, finally decided to cut his losses and pull the plug.

After Fang splintered, Bon stayed behind in London for a while, tending bar in a local pub. He and Irene, whose relationship had grown increasingly rocky, returned to Australia at the end of the year. An attempt to reconvene Fraternity on the group's home turf proved fruitless. Bon, at loose ends, got a job working at a fertilizer plant, while jamming informally with another Adelaide combo, the Mount Lofty Rangers.

One night in February 1974, after arguing with both Irene and the Rangers, a drunken Bon, whose long-standing propensity for dangerous trail-bike stunts had long ago won him the nickname Road Test Ronnie, crashed his Triumph motorcycle, suffering a broken collarbone, arm, leg and nose, severe facial lacerations and the loss of several teeth, topped off with a concussion. For three days he was in a coma and narrowly escaped death when his doctor restarted his stopped heart. After regaining consciousness, he spent four weeks in traction. Being laid up with a cast was no picnic for the free-spirited singer, who considered his mobility as essential as breathing. With his jaws wired shut, he had to drink his liquor through a straw.

Though he would bear scars and residual pain from the accident for the rest of his life, Bon bounced back from his injuries quickly. The remaining members of Fraternity took another stab at relaunching the band, but Bon wasn't thrilled with the prospect of reliving the disappointments and frustrations of the last three years.

Once he was back on his feet, Bon's old friend Vince Lovegrove, now based in Adelaide and writing about music for *Go-Set* and the *Adelaide News* as well as hosting a local TV pop show, gave him some odd jobs to keep him busy. In August, Lovegrove told Bon about a rising young Sydney band called AC/DC, which was looking to replace its lead singer.

7

SEND FOR THE MAN

By September 1974 Angus and Malcolm were champing at the bit to replace AC/DC's stack-heeled, leather-studded front-man, Dave Evans, with someone a bit more attuned to their musical wavelength. They had unsuccessfully attempted to lure John Paul Young—not a relative, but a Vanda/Young protégé who'd scored a few Australian hits and would later achieve short-lived U.S. success with the song "Love Is in the Air"—into the fold. But it wasn't until the Adelaide stop of the Lou Reed tour that a more appropriate candidate would muscle his way into the Young brothers' line of vision.

Vince Lovegrove had been aware that AC/DC was looking for a singer and had brought up Bon's name to George Young. But when George passed the suggestion on to nineteen-year-old Angus and twenty-one-year-old Malcolm, the pair initially deemed the twenty-eight-year-old Scott too long in the tooth for the job. Bon, however, had other ideas. After seeing the band play in Adelaide, he decided that AC/DC was exactly the tonic needed to revive both his stalled career and his flagging morale, and began actively campaigning for the gig.

The group has long perpetuated the story that they met Scott while employing him as a driver/roadie, but this would seem to be more fanciful mythmaking than historical fact. Indeed, Angus and Malcolm have long exercised a certain artistic license in telling their band's story, glossing over the less tidy details of AC/DC's history while conveniently minimizing the contributions of former band members and deposed business associates from the band's official biography.

Bon's own version, as expressed in an interview segment of the subsequent AC/DC concert film *Let There Be Rock,* was somewhat closer to the truth. "I knew their manager," Scott said. "I'd never seen the band before, I'd never even heard of AC/DC, and their manager said, just stand here, and the band comes on in two minutes, and there's this little guy, in a school uniform, going crazy, and I laughed. I took the opportunity to explain to them how much better I was than the drongo they had singing for them. So they gave me a chance to prove it, and there I was."

Bon was given the opportunity to prove himself at an informal rehearsal held at the home of his old Fraternity mate Bruce Howe. With Angus and Malcolm on guitars, Howe on bass and various other Fraternity members providing moral support, Scott—still hobbling from the effects of his bike crash but energized by his desire to join AC/DC—let loose and wowed all in attendance. He was offered the job on the spot.

Within a couple of weeks, Bon was in Sydney playing his first AC/DC concert, his only rehearsal being an informal preshow run-through. As Angus recalls, "For the first gig the only rehearsal we had was just sitting around an hour before the gig, pulling out every rock 'n' roll song we knew. When we finally got there, Bon downed about two bottles of Bourbon with dope, coke, speed, and says, 'Right, I'm ready,' and he was too. He was fighting fit. There was this immediate transformation and he was running around yelling at the audience. It was a magic moment."

In contrast to the rest of the band, who despite the time they'd spent slugging it out on the live circuit were relative innocents, AC/DC's new singer (whom they affectionately nicknamed the Old Man) had chalked up a wealth of hard-won experience, musical and otherwise. Besides, the worldly-wise Scott's carousing free-spiritedness seemed the perfect embodiment of the boisterous abandon that Angus and Malcolm wanted their band's music to convey.

Unlike the focused and relatively cautious Young brothers, who possessed the discipline to channel their rebelliousness into career ambition, Bon (who at 5´8˝ stood a full seven inches taller than either Young brother) was a genuine wild card—a grown-up juvenile delinquent with a lifestyle as reckless as his awesome vocal rasp, whose rakish charm and unassuming personal warmth often allowed him to escape the consequences of his sexual and alcoholic excesses. Paradoxically, Bon's wealth of performing experience made him a seasoned pro whose skills would serve as an inspiration to his new bandmates

"When I sang, I always felt that there was a certain amount of urgency to what I was doing," Bon explained. "There was no vocal training in my background, just a lot of good whiskey . . . I went through a period where I copied a lot of guys, and found when I was singing that I was starting to sound just like them. But when I met up with [AC/DC], they told me to sound like myself, and I really had a free hand doing what I always wanted to do.

"You get on that stage, and the more crass, gross and rowdy

you sound, the more they love it," he continued. "So I just go up there and scream away, sometimes to a point where I can't talk the next day."

Bon's arrival spurred an upsurge in AC/DC's spirits, thanks in equal parts to his performing abilities and his gung-ho enthusiasm. Impressed by the brothers' musical empathy as well as their single-minded drive to succeed, Bon was convinced that AC/DC possessed the goods to achieve what his previous bands couldn't, in both musical and career terms. In turn, the Young brothers drew inspiration from the relentless cheerleading of their new frontman, who was brimming with confidence in his new role—even if many of his old cronies thought he was selling out by involving himself in a band as willfully unpretentious as AC/DC.

Bon entered AC/DC at a crucial juncture. His first two months in the group included a grueling Australian tour, which served as a warm-up to the recording of the band's debut album. Though the pressure was on, trepidations quickly slipped away once the new lineup hit the stage. It was obvious that they were onto something special.

The addition of Scott was just the first in a wave of changes that would help make AC/DC a more professional, forward-looking outfit. Soon, the relatively small-time Dennis Laughlin—who'd been known to sit in with Fraternity prior to his involvement with AC/DC and who had on occasion been pressed into AC/DC frontman duty when Dave Evans was unavailable or unwanted—was out. In stepped Michael Browning, a Melbourne mover and shaker who owned that town's Hard Rock Cafe and who had just completed a five-year stint managing Australian rock vet Billy Thorpe and his band the Aztecs.

Browning recognized in AC/DC a distinct blend of credibility, professionalism and hardheaded ambition that was rare among Australian bands. After meeting with Browning, George Young found that Browning's vision of AC/DC coincided with his own—that the band possessed the goods to become the first Australian band since the Easybeats to achieve overseas stardom—and gave the thumbs-up to Browning's installation as manager.

By the mid-seventies the time finally seemed right for Australia to produce a world-class hard-rock act. The hippie haze of the sixties had faded, and heavy-metal pioneers like Led Zeppelin, Deep Purple and Black Sabbath were already established as arena-level acts, but those bands' grandiose presentation and aura of self-importance gave the average kid little to relate to. "Every time I ever saw a band," Angus said, "they seemed so untouchable they never seemed completely real. [We were] determined to stay away from that."

From the start, AC/DC's approach to its music and career emphasized the qualities of fun, straightforwardness and good old-fashioned hard work—qualities that stood in direct contrast to the condescending spectacle that had largely overtaken the music industry in the first half of the seventies. "[We] always thought we were in the first division, even when we were playing small clubs back in Australia," said Angus. "We never wanted to compete with the local bands—we wanted to compete with the world."

But before AC/DC could conquer the world, it would still need to conquer Australia, a goal it would continue to pursue through near-constant roadwork. That approach was a particularly draining one, given the punishing logistics of touring in Australia, whose urban population centers are separated by vast expanses of wilderness. It is a market that rewards only the hardiest, most imperturbable rockers. Fortunately for AC/DC, that's exactly what they were.

8

SHOOT TO THRILL

Among Michael Browning's initial acts as AC/DC's manager were paying off the band's considerable debts, securing a professional road crew, replacing the musicians' battered stage gear and relocating the band to Browning's base of Melbourne—which, as Australia's musical capital, offered substantially more opportunities for a young band than Sydney.

Upon arriving in Melbourne in December 1974, AC/DC quickly became a hit with local audiences, winning over pub and club crowds while blowing bigger-name headliners off the stage at larger shows. Living communally in a ratty old house in the Melbourne district of East St. Kilda, the band members more or less ran wild, enjoying many of the freedoms afforded red-blooded young men living away from home for the first time.

By the beginning of 1975, changes were afoot in AC/DC's rhythm section. Drummer Pete Clack was judged not to be cutting it rhythmically, while bassist Rob Bailey was reportedly sacked for the dual transgressions of being married and too tall. Into the drum seat almost immediately fell Phil Rudd—nee Rudzevecuis, born May 19, 1954, in Melbourne—who'd been beating the skins behind future Rose Tattoo frontman Angry Anderson in the Melbourne boogie outfit, Buster Brown.

The bass slot proved a bit tougher to fill, as Bon admitted to *RAM*. "It's a pretty rare type of bloke who'll fit into our band," he said. "He has to be under five feet six. And he has to be able to play bass pretty well too." Until a proper replacement could be found, AC/DC gigged as a quartet, with Malcolm holding down four-string duties.

When the band played at the annual Sunbury festival in January, though, it was as a five-piece, with George Young sitting in on bass. But that high-profile engagement was marred when the festival's headliners, Deep Purple, after much behind-the-scenes hubbub, decided that they didn't want AC/DC following them. When AC/DC attempted to take the stage while Purple's crew was clearing that band's gear, the resulting confrontation escalated into an onstage brawl—right in front of an audience of twenty thousand.

The English hard-rock titans' condescending treatment of AC/DC and the other Australian acts on the bill made it all the more clear to Michael Browning why AC/DC was going to have to make some serious commercial headway overseas if it was going to gain any respect.

Just before relocating to Melbourne—and a mere six weeks after Bon Scott joined the band—AC/DC had cut its first LP, *High Voltage,* with George Young and Harry Vanda sharing production credit. The eight-song album was, according to Angus, recorded "in ten days, in between gigs, working through the night after we came offstage and then through the day." Drummer Clack was deemed unsuitable for the job at hand and was replaced by studio player Tony Kerrante for the sessions; neither Clack nor Bailey (who were out of the picture by the time the disc hit the streets) was credited on the album.

Not surprisingly, considering its rushed origins, the finished album is something of a half-baked affair, with most of its compositions hastily cobbled together by matching Angus and Malcolm's long-completed but still wordless tunes with appropriate verbiage culled from Bon's backlogged lyric notebooks. But despite being a low-budget rush job by a band that had yet to fully coalesce, *High Voltage* captures a certain raucous spirit and gives some indication of what the early AC/DC's club gigs must have been like.

A frenzied cover of the blues standard "Baby Please Don't Go," long a staple of the band's live sets, kicked off the LP in fine style. The album's seven remaining tracks were all originals, with the bluesy six-and-a-half-minute "Soul Stripper" credited to Angus and Malcolm and the rest attributed to the Young brothers and Scott collectively. Other highlights included the slow grind of "Little Lover," the witty boogie of "Show Business" and the nasty, churning "She's Got Balls," whose lyrics were written by Bon in tribute to his semi-estranged wife, Irene.

In addition to acting as AC/DC's song publisher and production company, Albert Productions took control over releasing the band's product as well. Through a distribution deal with the Australian arm of the powerful EMI—whose connections would, they hoped, prove helpful to the band's efforts at gaining international distribution—the album appeared on the joint EMI/Albert label, but did not see release outside of Australia.

High Voltage and its first single, "Baby Please Don't Go," were released in February 1975 and entered the national charts the following month—probably more an indication of the Australian market's demand for AC/DC product than of the album's actual quality.

The album's release was followed by the addition of nineteen-year-old Melbourne native Mark Evans on bass. Despite the apocryphal anecdote about Bon meeting Mark after rescuing him from being pummeled by bouncers at an AC/DC gig, the more mundane truth is that Evans learned of the vacancy through a friend who was an AC/DC roadie.

Even at this early stage, Angus and Malcolm had developed a reputation for being unduly suspicious of outsiders, even fellow musicians, and this tendency—read, understandably, as arrogance by many observers—drew a certain amount of resentment within the Melbourne rock scene.

The brothers' attitude was the polar opposite of the friendly, unassuming Bon, whom they looked up to for his experience and street smarts. Bon, in turn, felt protective of the younger Youngs, who'd more or less salvaged his musical career. He also didn't seem to mind that most of the image-making hype applied by Michael Browning and the Albert organization stressed Angus as the group's visual focal point. But the siblings' insular fortress attitude, which would become more pronounced as the band became more successful, would eventually serve to distance Bon from Angus and Malcolm.

Another factor that would cause increasing friction between Scott and his bandmates was the singer's reckless live-for-the-moment approach to life, which in 1975 had already emerged as a cause for concern among those around him. His drinking, already excessive when he joined the band, was growing steadily more so, and his more recent dabblings in heroin, largely inspired by a junkie girlfriend, had resulted in a near-fatal overdose early in the year. Similarly life-threatening was the incident in which a seventeen-year-old female acquaintance's disapproving father showed up at the band's house with a couple of friends and gave the singer what he described as "the worst beating I have ever had," leaving him with a five hundred dollar dental bill.

But Bon also possessed a certain innocence, with a chivalrous streak that offset his rampant womanizing, and a genuine love for his work that allowed him to get away with his myriad excesses. At least initially, he felt liberated by his acceptance as a member of AC/DC. Heedless of the pain caused by his still-recent bike-crash injuries, he jumped into his new gig like a man who'd been given a new lease on life.

"Until I joined this band, I was always very frustrated," he said. "I had written songs, like 'She's Got Balls,' but in the band I was with, I was too scared to show 'em 'cause they was a bit more intelligent than I was. All of it comes down to frustration and anxiety. All those years of not being able to say what you wanted . . . Rock 'n' roll is the channel to give us all a vent to those frustrations. Lack of money, lack of women, lack of alcohol or whatever, rock 'n' roll is just a damn good outlet for what's hurtin' inside."

With Scott having helped to solidify the band's musical direction, AC/DC worked constantly, building a rabidly loyal audience and honing its strengths as an exhaustingly athletic live unit. At this point, their live sets were still a mix of original material (with music generally written by Angus and Malcolm, and lascivious lyrics provided by Bon) and hyped-up arrangements of blues, rock and R&B standards. "Baby Please Don't Go" was still the grand finale of AC/DC's live set, generally climaxing in Angus's tongue-in-cheek striptease and his piggyback ride into the audience on Bon's shoulders. Bon's stage antics would equal Angus's, with the singer regularly rolling around onstage, stripping naked, dressing in drag and engaging in good-natured lewdness of various stripes.

Although Angus's school uniform was already a fixture in the live show, he'd also experimented with a Zorro costume, a gorilla suit and even an improvised superhero persona dubbed Super Angus. "Bon was always trying to put me up to these crazy, wild ideas that spun in his head," Angus told *Rip* magazine. "I think it was his way of paying me back sometimes. I remember he locked me in a telephone box that we had on stage one night at [Sydney's] Hordern Pavilion. I was supposed to spring out of it. A roadie was going to let off a little explosion, but Bon, I think, paid him a few bucks to just put the explosion in front of him. Of course it went off, but not when it was supposed to."

One of the positive aspects of the confusion over the supposed sexual implications of AC/DC's name was that, not long after arriving in Melbourne, the band was embraced within the city's gay community. That distinction helped to create additional work opportunities for the band, which was a frequent featured attraction on Gay Nights at Browning's Hard Rock Cafe. "Upfront, bisexual women would come in and hold up vibrators," remembered Malcolm. "They had T-shirts on with holes cut out in front, and their boobs were poking through. It was great."

"I used to get offered parts in these strip places," Angus adds. "I did one once when I was a bit stuck up for money. I hopped onstage in the school uniform and stood there while this girl did a little dance."

"The she was a he anyway," Bon pointed out.

With "Baby Please Don't Go" becoming a minor hit single, AC/DC appeared on the influential Melbourne-based national TV show *Countdown,* hosted by Australian pop personality

Molly Meldrum. That appearance helped win the band a new set of younger female fans, who apparently viewed Bon and Angus as unconventional sex symbols.

In June 1975 the band released a non-LP single, "High Voltage Rock 'n' Roll" (originally written for the *High Voltage* album but not completed in time). The single coincided with a show at Melbourne's Festival Hall, at which Stevie Wright and John Paul Young served as support acts. AC/DC's set was shot by a four-camera film crew, for the purpose of producing a promotional video clip to be used by management in its attempts to raise overseas record company interest in the band. As if any further acknowledgment was necessary, this show served official notice that AC/DC had, in an impressively short time, climbed to the top of the rock heap in the group's adopted hometown.

9

SHOW BUSINESS

With Melbourne having fallen under AC/DC's spell, a move back to Sydney was next on the band's agenda. There, the quintet spent much of July 1975 ensconced in Albert Productions' new in-house studio recording their second LP, *TNT*. Bon would often still be writing his lyrics as the rest of the band was recording the instrumental tracks, with Angus shaking and jumping around the studio as if he were onstage. In fact, the band would generally lay its tracks down live in the studio, with guitar solos and vocals overdubbed.

If *High Voltage* had been a tentative if encouraging first step, *TNT,* released in Australia in February 1976, was as explosive as its title, boasting stronger performances and a more solidly defined stylistic direction rooted in Angus and Malcolm's fiercely interlocking guitar telepathy. The opening one-two punch of "It's a Long Way to the Top (If You Wanna Rock 'n' Roll)" and "Rock 'n' Roll Singer" offered a glimpse into the band's boundless ambition. Bon's gift for wordplay was in force on the loping, lascivious "The Jack" (whose title is Australian slang for venereal disease) and on bracingly upbeat declarations like "Live Wire," "T.N.T.," "Rocker" and the pre-LP single "High Voltage." Rounding out the album were a newly recorded version of "Can I Sit Next to You Girl" and an AC/DC-fied reading of Chuck Berry's "School Day."

By all accounts, at this stage George Young was largely responsible for hammering his brothers' spare riffs and melodic ideas into full-fledged songs. Angus later explained how George would ride herd over the band's raw compositions: "He'd take our meanest song and try it out on keyboards with arrangements like 10cc or even Mantovani. If it was passed, the structure was proven, then we took it away and dirtied it up."

In September 1975 AC/DC played a free concert at Sydney's Victoria Park. The same month, the first in a series of scheduled free lunchtime AC/DC shows at a Sydney department store erupted into a riot when the stage was rushed by several hundred shrieking teenage females. Not much later, after several fans started kicking Angus, Phil Rudd stepped in and sustained a broken thumb. The injury forced the band to call in ex-member Colin Burgess as a short-term replacement.

On New Year's Day 1976 AC/DC played a show in Adelaide, where a minor riot resulted after the band's power was cut and Bon incited the crowd to rush the stage. Bon was reported to have been seen in the ensuing melee in the crowd, riding on someone's shoulders and playing bagpipes.

Bagpipes would also figure in the band's next venture into the still-unfamiliar area of music video, in a clip they shot of "It's a Long Way to the Top" for *Countdown,* in which the band played on a flatbed truck as it drove through Melbourne, accompanied by three men playing bagpipes. The imagery was a nice nod to Bon's childhood experiences with Scottish pipe bands.

By the time *TNT* was released in February 1976—precisely a year after *High Voltage*—AC/DC was as popular in its home country as any international act. *TNT* sold eleven thousand copies in Australia during its first week of release, and both of the group's albums had topped the Australian sales charts while achieving silver, gold and platinum status, thanks in large part to the nearly two years' worth of unstinting road-work.

But, while their popularity in Australia was growing at a faster rate than the band could have anticipated, AC/DC's attempts to achieve international recognition had thus far failed to bear fruit. If anything, the group's success at home intensified its drive to expand into outside territories and explore uncharted ground. But if AC/DC was to make a significant long-term impression on overseas markets, it would need the support of a powerful record company with the experience and marketing clout to match the band's ambition.

Michael Browning found that support in the London office of the U.S.-based Atlantic Records, which had demonstrated an impressive knack for selling hard rock with late-sixties groups like England's Cream and America's Iron Butterfly and Vanilla Fudge, and had subsequently ushered in the age of modern heavy metal by signing and nurturing Led Zeppelin. Already impressed by AC/DC's achievements in its homeland, Atlantic's U.K. managing director, Phil Carson, signed the band to a worldwide contract.

With a British tour (and a possible subsequent U.S. trip)

The young Angus in action. He would soon be able to afford more reliable socks. *(Michael Putland, Retna)*

in the offing, it was determined that AC/DC should cut another album immediately, since finding time to write and
record new material might become difficult once overseas
touring commitments kicked in. So the band completed the
nine-song *Dirty Deeds Done Dirt Cheap* at Albert headquar-
ters in February 1976, the same month that *TNT* was released.
Once finished, the tapes were put on the shelf, to be unleashed
when new product was needed.

10

LIVE WIRE

Having soundly conquered Australia with *High Voltage* and *TNT,* there was little more for AC/DC to achieve on its home turf. If the band was to continue to grow, it would need to establish a foothold in foreign markets.

The next territory that AC/DC set its sights upon was Britain. England was the cradle of seventies hard rock, having spawned the influential heavy-metal triumvirate of Led Zeppelin, Black Sabbath and Deep Purple. To Angus, Malcolm and Bon, British expatriates as well as uncompromising rockers, England must have possessed special significance beyond pragmatic career considerations.

As geographical isolation had been a traditional source of frustration for Australian bands seeking to break into Western markets, it was decided that AC/DC would have a better shot at breaking internationally if the group was based in England, whose relative proximity to Europe and North America would render the logistics of international touring considerably less punishing. So it was that in April 1976 AC/DC dutifully picked up stakes and headed for London. On the eve of their departure, the band played an Australian farewell show for a packed house at the band's longtime Sydney haunt the Lifesaver; that evening reportedly marked the first time Angus ever mooned an audience.

"Success [in Australia] means nothing," Angus would later tell the English music weekly *Record Mirror,* with more than a trace of bitterness. "We left on a peak rather than overstaying our welcome."

AC/DC left Australia under the impression that it would be spending most of April and May touring the U.K. as opening act for former Free guitarist Paul Kossoff's band Back Street Crawler, who also recorded for Atlantic and shared the same British booking agency, Headline Artists. While AC/DC was en route to England, however, Kossoff's long history of heroin use finally caught up with him. By the time the band's plane landed, the much-troubled axeman was dead. As Bon wrote in a mock-angry missive to *RAM,* "That cunt Paul Kossoff fucked up our first tour. Wait'll Angus gets hold of him."

Stuck in a strange land for two months with no work lined up, AC/DC accepted the few pub and club gigs it could scrape up. It was a less-than-auspicious beginning for their ambitious assault on the British Isles, but it was consistent with the approach the band had always taken in Australia—playing wherever and whenever they could. It wouldn't be long before the wisdom of that philosophy would make itself clear once again.

Shortly after the group's arrival in London, Bon paid a visit to the pub in Finchley where he'd tended bar during Fraternity's latter days, and returned home with a dislocated jaw and a black eye. Apparently, just seconds after entering the establishment, Scott was hit in the face with a pint mug by someone with a long memory and a score to settle. This explains why, in AC/DC's first British photo session, Scott is seen wearing shades.

On May 14 Atlantic's British division released an AC/DC album entitled *High Voltage,* which despite its moniker was basically the Australian *TNT* with two tracks from the original *High Voltage,* "She's Got Balls" and "Little Lover," substituted for "Rocker" and "School Day." Though the compilation's first U.K. single, "It's a Long Way to the Top," didn't make much of an impression on the charts, the album did win the band a fair amount of media attention; one early supporter was renowned BBC Radio One DJ John Peel. Though U.K. reviews of *High Voltage* ran the gamut from admiration to disdain, Geoff Barton's four-star rave in *Sounds* boded well for the future, calling the music "a tonic in the midst of the all-too-serious poker-faced groups of today."

AC/DC's emergence on the London scene during the unusually hot English summer of 1976 coincided with both the hoopla surrounding the queen's upcoming Royal Jubilee celebration and the early stirrings of the punk-rock explosion.

Without the benefit of the media saturation that punk had going for it, AC/DC understood that establishing a niche in the British market would depend on building a grassroots following through live work. That strategy would prove quite effective, since English audiences had never experienced anything quite like AC/DC's uncompromising live attack—and almost invariably responded enthusiastically. For the band, the spectacle—encompassing the seemingly absurd juxtaposition of Angus's schoolboy garb and manic gesticulating, Bon's piercing shriek and sporadic bagpipe playing and the band's overwhelming roar—was all in a night's work, but for Londoners it was a completely new experience that was every bit as over-the-top as anything in punk, and louder to boot.

One such occasion was an unadvertised last-minute gig at a pub in Hammersmith called the Red Cow. In the time between the band's two sets, the ten or so people who'd attended the early show had apparently been so blown away that they ran out and dragged all their friends back in time for AC/DC to play its late set to a packed house of new converts.

The unlikely Red Cow triumph led to a successful run at London's more prestigious Nashville Rooms, during which one of the band's incendiary sets led Phil McNeill of the largely punk-aligned English music weekly *New Musical Express* to observe admiringly, "In the middle of the great British Punk Rock Explosion, a quintet of similarly ruthless Ozzies has just swaggered like a cat among London's surly, self-consciously paranoid pigeons . . . and with a sense of what sells rather than what's cool, they could well clean up. . . . We're impressed."

When Back Street Crawler, with a new guitarist stepping in for the late Paul Kossoff, feebly attempted to restart its postponed tour, AC/DC was back in tow as support band. The demoralizing trek, which included a high-profile show at London's legendary Marquee, ended up being canceled halfway through, but not before AC/DC had proved its mettle by consistently stealing the thunder from the bereaved headliners. It was obvious that AC/DC was more than ready to headline its own U.K. shows.

But first came the "Lock Up Your Daughters" tour, a twenty-date summer excursion put together by *Sounds,* on which AC/DC's fifty-minute live set was part of a program featuring a live DJ and film clips of other bands. The package met with a mixed response, but did include a successful July 7 stop at the London Lyceum, hosted by John Peel. After the show,

Bon pulled one of his patented disappearing acts, failing to show up for his own postgig thirtieth-birthday bash. The singer, who'd apparently sought company away from his bandmates, did not reappear until three days later.

Later in July, the band returned to the Marquee for a short but successful Monday-night residency, which consistently attracted enthusiastic capacity crowds. The Marquee run signified AC/DC's real breakthrough: the band was now recognized by London cognoscenti as a one-of-a-kind live act. As the club's manager, Jack Berry, commented to an Australian journalist, "AC/DC are the most exciting thing I've seen play at the Marquee since Led Zeppelin. The band is very original, not so much in what they do but in the way they do it. They are obviously tremendously talented and one can see from watching them that they are capable of playing to very large audiences."

The Marquee gigs firmly established AC/DC as virtually the only nonpunk band doing anything exciting in London in 1976. They attracted still more praise from the usually circumspect *New Musical Express:* "The only sound coming through the wall was chunka-chunka-chunka, while the bar resounded with ribald Aussies telling me to watch for Angus Young to expose himself. When he stripped off to his knickers and leapt on an amp a well-informed source wrinkled its nose and said, 'My God, he's been wearing the same underpants for four weeks.' "

Another *NME* writer subsequently lamented, "The only thing that brings me down is that they are getting too big to play clubs for very much longer. The immediacy of seeing them close up, no matter how wet and sticky it is, is dynamite. That's rock and roll. Screw paying four quid to see the old men in stadia; you've got to see AC/DC."

As it happened, AC/DC would have little trouble translating its ability to connect with crowds from clubs to larger venues, and the group would get the chance sooner than it expected. "We're absolutely stoked with what is going on here," Bon raved at the time. "We're progressing a lot faster than we'd expected, and it looks like we'll all be staying in England for a while yet, though we're all pretty homesick."

The band's Australian fans, meanwhile, had to settle for a new single, "Jailbreak," a track from the still-unreleased *Dirty Deeds Done Dirt Cheap* album, which continued to languish in Albert's vaults waiting for *TNT*'s massive Australian sales to abate, which they gave little indication of doing.

The band topped off a very encouraging summer with an appearance at England's Reading Rock Festival, in front of a crowd numbering fifty thousand. Reading is an honored institution in British rock; a successful appearance there can be instrumental in launching a career. Unfortunately, AC/DC's set was something of a misfire, apparently due more to an unenthusiastic crowd than a substandard performance.

At least Angus got to drop his pants. "All of a sudden this girl with enormous tits walked past the stage at the front. Everything seemed to stop as the whole mesmerized crowd watched this massive pair wander past. So I dropped my trousers."

With British audiences bowing to the band's will, AC/DC set its sights on Europe, undertaking a nineteen-date tour of the Continent, supporting ex–Deep Purple guitar star Ritchie Blackmore's new band, Rainbow; the tour was preceded by three headlining gigs in Germany, where the *High Voltage* compilation had sold sixteen thousand copies in its first week of release. Though touring with Rainbow should have been a perfect opportunity for AC/DC to play for enthusiastic hard-rock fans, Blackmore's fabled peevishness made the trip something less than fulfilling. True to his reputation as one of hard rock's most volatile hotheads, the ever-brooding Blackmore made it clear that he was not happy to see the opening act stealing his thunder.

"One night in Munich," Malcolm recalled, "the audience wanted us back for an encore. Because it was Blackmore's show, we couldn't go back on. And they put the house lights out, and people stood up with their lighters flickering. Half the audience walked out during Blackmore's set."

Blackmore would subsequently show up at an AC/DC show at the Marquee in London, where he reportedly confided to an acquaintance that he considered the group to be "the lowest form of rock 'n' roll around." But AC/DC got its revenge, albeit unwittingly. Malcolm: "The Marquee's manager had asked him if he'd get up onstage and jam with us at the end of our set. We'd just finished, and Angus was exhausted. Blackmore grabbed a guitar and got up onstage. But we'd come off and we didn't know he was there. We just went home, and he was left standing there like an idiot! He's put in a bad word for us, so let's straighten it out, eh? We actually think he's the oldest form of low in rock 'n' roll."

Even at this early stage, through either their lyrical subject matter or their personal behavior, or more likely a combination of both, AC/DC had already cultivated a powerful aura of licentiousness. "The only image we've ever had is what we really are," stated Angus. "We never cover anything. I mean, if Bon's kissing a virgin down the room and someone spots him, well, tough shit. Nobody can blackmail him."

That reputation would quickly come back to haunt the band on the string of U.K. dates that it undertook after finishing the Rainbow tour. The tour was to include a dozen shows, many of them at colleges, but the band's reputation caused certain authority figures to blanch at the thought of AC/DC sullying the hallowed halls of higher education. For instance, they were refused permission to perform at Oxford Polytechnic because of their songs' "sexism and cheap jokes" and their "blatantly vulgar and cheap references to both sexes."

AC/DC wouldn't need to play college gigs much longer anyway, as demonstrated by a show at London's four-thousand-seat Hammersmith Odeon. Even though the venue was only about half full, the crowd's rabid reaction made it clear that the band was destined for big things. As the *NME* noted, "The schoolboy brat on the rostrum smirks maliciously as his opening power chord painfully rattles through our bones and makes the unnecessary triumphant gesture of wildly tossing his cap to the floor, as if to say 'This is the day, the day, gawd 'elp us all, AC/DC conquered London.' "

The *London Times,* meanwhile, was less enthusiastic, but—unlike most of the band's critics—didn't fault the band's risqué lyrics. "My objections are to their music, not their words, which simply express without inhibitions what most of us have discussed innumerable times with equal frankness in private," wrote the respectable daily. "Music of any sort must surely require more from performers than just the capacity to mindlessly bash their instruments into oblivion. It is in this primal state that AC/DC exist."

11
RIFF RAFF

The punk movement charged mainstream rock with having grown lazy and lost touch with the rebellious energy that was its original source of inspiration. Driven by the same youthful frustration that had originally fueled early rock 'n' roll, many punks recognized what they and AC/DC had in common.

Though punk's emphasis on raw-edged aggression and musical simplicity did indeed have much in common with their own no-frills, in-your-face aesthetic, Angus and Malcolm Young despised punk, which they derided as a self-conscious fad driven by media hype and controlled by middle-class intellectuals. Therefore, they took extreme umbrage when media observers persisted in identifying the staunchly working-class, rabidly anti-analytical AC/DC with the punk movement.

"It's very easy to become an instantly controversial band," Angus later scoffed. "The Sex Pistols proved that it's easy to achieve instant stardom, but they couldn't play anywhere and they broke up. The punk-rock thing has much more to do with fashion than rock 'n' roll music. [AC/DC] is a hardworking, working-class band—we're not former art school students like a lot of punk rockers."

Despite the Young brothers' unconcealed disdain for punk, AC/DC had far more in common with punk's anarchic spirit than they cared to admit. In its early days in London, the band often shared U.K. club bills with punk bands, and it's to AC/DC's credit that its act was uncompromisingly obnoxious enough to be accepted by punk fans. But as Angus and Malcolm instinctively understood, AC/DC's real constituency would be kids who were tired of mainstream rock's bloated self-importance yet not comfortable with punk's confrontational, politicized stance.

Angus and Malcolm's protests aside, AC/DC was ideally suited to bridge the gap between the naked aggression of hard rock and punk's pared-down melodic drive, as demonstrated by the group's popularity with the readers of *Sounds.* Unlike its punk-leaning weekly counterparts *Melody Maker* and *New Musical Express,* the more populist *Sounds* balanced its support of punk with an equal predilection for heavy metal. In an end-of-year readers' poll to pick rock's "new order," AC/DC led the pack, followed by Eddie and the Hot Rods, the Sex Pistols, the Damned, Iggy Pop, Ted Nugent, Ritchie Blackmore's Rainbow, Motorhead, Judas Priest, the Ramones and the Dictators.

Bon Scott, who wasn't quite as intolerant of other musical styles as the Youngs, could still make a persuasive case for AC/DC's stylistic tunnel vision, as he did in an interview with *RAM.* "You play what you were brought up on, what you believe in," he said. "I can listen to other bands that play really intricate stuff and I can appreciate it, and I even like some of it, but I'd never attempt to play it."

AC/DC returned to Australia in late November for a twenty-six-date homecoming tour, which was briefly interrupted by a jaunt back to London for a triumphant one-night stand at Hammersmith Odeon; the band's Christmas shows would subsequently become something of a tradition for AC/DC's London fans. While the band was still promoting *High Voltage* in the Northern Hemisphere, the Australian dates coincided with the Christmas release of their long-completed third album, *Dirty Deeds Done Dirt Cheap,* which would not reach U.S. shelves for another five years.

The album kicked off with the title track, which featured a cartoonishly nasty lyric as well as the band's catchiest chorus to date. "I came up with the title," beamed Angus. "I got it from the cartoon *Beany and Cecil.* There was this guy Dishonest John and he had a card that said, 'Dirty Deeds Done Cheap. Holidays, Sundays and Special Rates.' "

Equally impressive was the rousing "Jailbreak" (accompanied by an impressive promo video whose conceptual elements predated MTV by several years), whose lyrical metaphor of imprisonment and liberation drew on Bon's experiences with incarceration; and the equally autobiographical "Ain't No Fun (Waiting Around to Be a Millionaire)." Elsewhere, Bon applied his best vocal leer for the vengeful lyrics of "Squealer" and the goofy spoken-word double entendres of "Big Balls," while the rockabilly-styled "Rocker" offered an appreciative nod to his fifties rock 'n' roll influences. "Problem Child" ranked with the band's most persuasive bad-boy anthems, while the band gamely (if weakly) attempted a bluesy stroll on "Ride On."

When *Dirty Deeds Done Dirt Cheap* was released in Britain, it was with an altered track sequence that omitted "Jailbreak" and "Rock in Peace" in favor of "Rocker," a *TNT* number omitted from the U.S./U.K. *High Voltage,* and "Love at First Feel," a new song that the band would release as a single in Australia in January 1977.

Meanwhile, the Australian tour, which marked AC/DC's return home after an eight-month absence, saw the group welcomed as conquering heroes, greeted by a small but passionate throng of screaming girls at the airport. Though the opening gig of the Australian tour, at Melbourne's Myer Music Bowl, was an unqualified triumph, it wasn't long before the tour was beset by controversy. The first sign of trouble occurred at the second show, in the Victoria/New South Wales border town of Albury, where the band had to stop selling its tour program because the local town clerk had made a fuss over one of Bon's spicier quotes.

That tempest in a teacup was only the first in a series of protests and local bans that would plague the "Giant Dose of Rock 'n' Roll" tour. The following night, the band was warned that the plug would be pulled if Angus were to expose his increasingly notorious bottom. Later, the mayor of Tamworth refused to grant permission for the band to play in his town, forcing cancellation of that show. Further, radio station 2SM, one of the band's earliest media supporters, announced that it would no longer broadcast AC/DC records or advertise the band's shows (the ban may have had something to do with the fact that the station was owned by the Catholic Church).

These were followed by several more miniature media controversies, like female fans who were supposedly running out and getting tattoos in tribute to Bon, or the widow who supposedly began receiving obscene phone calls because her number was the same as the "36-24-36" mentioned in "Dirty Deeds Done Dirt Cheap." Meanwhile, a member of Australia's Parliament officially expressed concerns over the band threatening the morals of the nation's youth.

One frequent focus for public outrage was Angus's oft-exposed rear end. As Bon quipped to *RAM*, "You see his backside in the papers more than you see his face—which is preferential as far as I'm concerned."

Due to these controversies, along with disappointing turnouts in several venues, the Australian tour was something less than the homecoming triumph it should have been. The misguided stirrings of petty moral outrage further soured AC/DC on the Australian market; they would scale back their activities there in the future. After experiencing the professionalism of the British music industry, the band had little patience for the relative backwater amateurism of the Australian circuit.

At one show, at Miami High School Great Hall on Australia's Gold Coast, AC/DC was supported by the Saints, whose then-current single "(I'm) Stranded" had pretty much single-handedly launched an Australian punk movement. Needless to say, the Young brothers didn't like them.

Threats from the city fathers of the Victorian mining town of Warrnambool to ban the group from playing its scheduled January 12 show there proved to be the last straw for the band's rapidly thinning patience. A newspaper report, headlined "Rock Band Threatens to Leave Country," read, "AC/DC—Australia's raunchiest rock group—have threatened to quit the country and settle in England because of alleged 'hounding' from local authorities." The story quoted Angus as saying, "It's no good if we drive halfway across the country to stage a concert to find out that someone has canceled it because they consider us obscene. It will only take a couple more hassles from the authorities and we will leave Australia."

Angus's threat was somewhat disingenuous, actually, since AC/DC had more or less abandoned Australia already, to concentrate on more lucrative territories like America, where the hybrid *High Voltage* had been released in October 1976 to a familiar love-it-or-hate-it response. The U.S. music-industry trade journal *Billboard* called it "a cross between Led Zeppelin and the Sensational Alex Harvey Band," noting that the "lead singer has a very unique sounding voice and the twin guitars are front and center from the first cut."

Rolling Stone, however, was unequivocal in its contempt for the band's rowdy attack. "Those concerned with the future of hard rock may take solace in knowing that with the release of the first U.S. album by these Australian gross-out champions, the genre has unquestionably hit its all-time low," wrote critic Billy Altman. "Lead singer Bon Scott spits out his vocals with a truly annoying aggression which, I suppose, is the only way to do it when all you seem to care about is being a star so that you can get laid every night."

Although the *High Voltage* compilation had sold encouragingly in the U.K. and Europe, where the band was judged to be on the verge of a major commercial breakthrough, AC/DC's future in the U.S. market looked considerably less rosy. The group's initial plans to tour America in late 1976 had been scuttled by its failure to gain visas due to Bon's criminal record. And with no live performances to build a stateside reputation on, the band's American profile was virtually nonexistent.

Atlantic's U.S. division was unimpressed by *High Voltage's* lackluster domestic sales and showed little interest in issuing further AC/DC product. They'd already passed on *Dirty Deeds Done Dirt Cheap* in the States—partly because they'd released *High Voltage* just a few months prior, but also because they objected to the album's sloppy production. In fact, Atlantic came close to dropping AC/DC in the U.S.; it was only through the urgings of U.K. supporter Phil Carson that the band managed to keep its place on the label's roster.

12

DOG EAT DOG

After finishing the tour, AC/DC remained in Australia to record its fourth album with Harry Vanda and George Young, in the now-familiar environment of the Albert studio. Just a few months earlier, Vanda and Young had returned to the Australian and European pop charts as artists, using the punning nom de disc Flash and the Pan, with the international hit "Hey St. Peter!"

Though the sessions were once again rushed to slot in with the group's touring commitments, the resulting album, *Let There Be Rock,* would easily emerge as AC/DC's strongest work to date. In addition to noticeably upgraded production values, the eight-song collection featured sharp, streamlined performances that demonstrated how far the band had progressed since its arrival in England.

Alongside the pummeling, anthemic title track were such quintessentially rebellious autobiographical statements as

"Bad Boy Boogie," "Dog Eat Dog," "Hell Ain't a Bad Place to Be" and "Problem Child" (the latter salvaged from the Australian *Dirty Deeds Done Dirt Cheap* for *Let There Be Rock*'s U.S. edition). Bon's flair for the lascivious first-person vignette was as compelling as ever on "Go Down," inspired by noted groupie Ruby Lips, and "Whole Lotta Rosie," a tribute to a large-framed female fan whom the ever-randy vocalist once bedded as a challenge from his bandmates. Perhaps most telling, though, was "Overdose," on which Bon sings with an immediacy that gives added resonance to the song's sex-as-addiction metaphor.

It was during the *Let There Be Rock* sessions that several colorful, if apocryphal, anecdotes arose illustrating the band's recording methods. One such item involves Angus overdubbing a guitar solo when billows of smoke began pouring from his amp, while George Young gestured for Angus to continue playing. "There was no way we were going to stop a shit-hot performance for a technical reason like amps blowing up!" the elder Young supposedly commented.

After a few more gigs in Sydney, Melbourne and Adelaide, AC/DC returned to the U.K. in February 1977 to begin a twenty-six-date British tour. The British dates were followed by a tension-riddled trip to Europe supporting Black Sabbath, whose grandiose pretensions must have provided a wicked contrast for AC/DC's aggressively unpretentious approach. Even worse, the Sabs, who just a few years earlier had been one of metal's mightiest juggernauts, were by now enfeebled by drug use.

On the road, tensions ran high between the two bands—tensions that were undoubtedly exacerbated by the fact that AC/DC was widely reported to be blowing the headliners off the stage every night. At one point, a member of Sabbath reportedly pulled a knife on Malcolm Young and the confrontation erupted into a fistfight, providing all the excuse the Sabs needed to boot AC/DC from the tour. Their premature exit aside, the tour saw AC/DC getting the strongest responses it had ever received from European audiences.

By now, AC/DC were old hands at stealing headliners' thunder. "We never used to consider ourselves as supporting this band or that band," explained Angus. "We were playing, that's how we always thought of it. When we went onstage, it was our stage and we didn't care whose name was at the top of the bill . . . We just get out there and rock. If your amp blows up or your guitar packs it in, smash it up and pick another one. And that's how it always was with us.

"We could go on and just be dead bland and not try and involve the audience in anything, but you may as well just play like on the record and not bother to try anything new. We get most of our ideas for songs when we're playing live . . . Every now and then we'll just blow, and me, by accident, I'll learn something new."

"We're on the crowd's side because we give 'em what they want," stated Bon. "It's a band/audience show. We're not like performing seals, we're all in it together."

Indeed, the raucous drive of AC/DC's live show was consistently underscored by a genuine desire to give its fans value for money. "We can't just sit on our arses and say the world owes us a livin' because we've paid our dues," said Angus. "Me, I think if I fluff a note I'm robbin' the kids. You've gotta pour it all on until you drop. So even if they hate you, they can still say, 'At least they tried.' "

In the spring of 1977 *Let There Be Rock* became AC/DC's first simultaneous worldwide release. Its startlingly impressive quality, which finally managed to focus all of AC/DC's most compelling qualities into one concise package, rendered the relatively primitive *Dirty Deeds Done Dirt Cheap*—which still had yet to be released in the U.S.—obsolete.

Both for the band's fans and the band itself, *Let There Be Rock* was the album on which AC/DC truly came into its own, with upgraded material, performances and sonic dynamics, not to mention an overall atmosphere that better reflected the immediacy of the band's live performances. As such, it became the blueprint for all of the AC/DC albums to come.

The album's biblically intoned title might have served as a red flag to those self-appointed guardians of public morality who would soon be accusing AC/DC of being in league with satanic forces. A more significant feature of the *Let There Be Rock* package, though, was the debut appearance of the now-familiar AC/DC "lightning bolt" logo.

While the album was released to better reviews and encouraging sales figures, the majority of critics still regarded AC/DC as a reactionary tool of rock's bloated old guard rather than the vanguard of an exciting musical future. Andy Gill, reviewing a Sheffield concert for the *NME*, dismissed the quintet as "4/4 monotony sexists led by a snot-nosed brat."

By now, though, the band was immune to such criticism, as Bon made clear. "The music press is totally out of touch with what the kids actually want to listen to," he said. "These kids might be working in a shitty factory all week, or they might be on the dole. Come the weekend, they just want to go out and have a good time, get drunk and go wild. We give them the opportunity to do that."

Reviewing an AC/DC show in Sheffield, England, the *NME*'s John Hamblett attempted to put the band's obvious appeal in perspective, describing the audience as "young, post-hippy, post-acid, post-love and peace . . . all hungry for a two-hour slice of the sex and drugs and rock 'n' roll dream cake.

Not one of them looks like he or she gives a solitary damn about any pie-in-the-sky abstract questions of social relevance or contemporariness. Hell, why should they? They've got real problems crowding up their heads, like what to do with Saturday night to make the rest of the week bearable," adding that "AC/DC, the outrageous Aussies, [play] the only type of music that could conceivably gell with this outside, desperate, good-time atmosphere: blistering and warping electric waves of hard-nose music, a mish-mash of the most unholy influences imaginable."

Let There Be Rock's release was followed closely by the surprise departure of bassist Mark Evans, who up until that point had generally been regarded as AC/DC's best-behaved, most even-tempered member. Though the official line was that Evans had grown weary of the rigors of the road and that the split had been amicable, the truth, according to insiders, was that Evans had become something of a scapegoat for the Young brothers' myriad career frustrations. For his trouble, Evans reportedly walked away with a paltry $2,000, which he'd been talked into accepting in exchange for his rights to all future royalties on the band's albums.

It is claimed by some that, at the time, the Young brothers were ready to give the boot to Bon Scott as well. Apparently, the band's American record company, finally seeing AC/DC's commercial potential thanks to *Let There Be Rock*'s musical potency, was concerned about Scott's general reliability. Though Bon got to keep his job, Mark Evans's dismissal was taken by many in the know as an indication of the Young brothers' determination not to let anything stand in the way of AC/DC's all-out assault on the U.S. market.

According to myth, new bassist Cliff Williams had been recruited through a musician-wanted ad placed in the British music papers. Actually, he was suggested to Browning by a mutual friend. At twenty-eight, Williams—born on December 17, 1949, in Romford, England—had already been playing music for a decade and a half. Growing up in Liverpool, Williams had worked with a succession of bands and was playing with an obscure outfit known as Bandit when he received the call from AC/DC.

The fact that the relatively stable, centered Williams was closer in age and background to Scott was a positive development for Bon, who, on a social level, seemed increasingly alienated from the rest of the band. In social situations with fellow AC/DC members, he'd regularly wander off to enjoy the less-demanding company of fans and female admirers.

By the summer of 1977 AC/DC had solidly established itself as an undeniable presence in the British and European markets. Now, after a panoply of delays, it was finally time for the band to set its sights on the biggest game of all—America.

13

THERE'S GONNA BE SOME ROCKIN'

Although AC/DC's only prior U.S. release had sold unexceptionally, the obvious quality of *Let There Be Rock* reawakened the interest of Atlantic's American division, particularly new execs Perry Cooper and Michael Klenfner, who were confident that the band's boozy, high-energy attack would be embraced by an eager audience in the U.S. once the band received the opportunity to strut its stuff in stateside venues.

The band couldn't have agreed more. As Bon told David Fricke in *Circus*, "There's been an audience waiting for an honest rock 'n' roll band to come along and lay it on 'em. There's a lot of people coming out of the woodwork to see our kind of rock. And they're not the same people who would go to see James Taylor or a punk band."

"We've got the basic thing the kids want," said Angus. "They want to rock, and that's it. They want to be part of this band as a mass. When you hit a guitar chord, a lot of the kids

in the audience are hitting it with you. They're so much into the band, they're going through all the motions with you. If you can get the mass to react as a whole, then that's the ideal thing. That's what a lot of bands lack, and why the critics are wrong."

Although the band would soon be wowing American audiences firsthand, it would become abundantly clear that conquering a territory as large and diffuse as the United States was going to require substantial investments of time and energy. Although the band had managed to amass a following in the two markets—Jacksonville, Florida, and Columbus, Ohio—where *High Voltage* had received airplay, Atlantic and manager Browning (who by this point had set up an office in New York to better facilitate his efforts on the band's behalf) understood that AC/DC's chances of gaining mainstream radio airplay were remote and that a U.S. breakthrough would depend on the band's willingness to tour incessantly.

After a short spate rehearsing in Sydney with new bassist Williams, AC/DC arrived in the U.S. in June 1977, playing a successful string of club dates between Texas and Florida, where it was hoped that audiences weaned on southern gutbucket boogie would be responsive to AC/DC's straight-to-the-gut attack. That leg climaxed with a triumphant gig in Jacksonville, Florida—which at this point was the group's strongest American market—sharing the bill with REO Speedwagon and Pat Travers in front of a packed house of eight thousand.

The band made a double-edged New York debut on August 24, playing a well-received set as opening act for the Dictators—the Big Apple punk scene's rudest cartoon toughs—at

---

Angus in maximum overdrive. *[Michael Putland, Retna]*

New York's Palladium, before heading downtown to the now-legendary punk mecca CBGB's, where they performed for an uncomprehending crowd on a bill headlined by the now-forgotten Marbles.

From New York, the band flew to the West Coast for a series of arena dates with Ted Nugent, followed by a series of headlining club gigs including four well-received shows at San Francisco's Old Waldorf club and one sparsely attended night at L.A.'s Whisky A-Go-Go. After the latter event, Bon Scott and Phil Rudd took a day trip to Disneyland, where their fun was curtailed by the fact that the joints they'd brought along were, unbeknownst to them, spiked with angel dust.

The band's characteristic cockiness aside, AC/DC was somewhat overwhelmed and intimidated by the vastness of America. Nonetheless, the group spent much of the summer of 1977 traversing the country, building an audience base virtually from the ground up. Crowds responded enthusiastically to such by-now-time-tested gimmicks as Angus's demented-schoolboy routine and his nightly "walkabout" into the audience on Bon's shoulders—not to mention Angus's new prop book bag, which emitted clouds of smoke.

The U.S. dates also saw the debut of Angus's new wireless guitar setup as well, replacing the long guitar cords he'd been using thus far; the transmitter allowed Angus to wander the stage with no encumbrances. "When I used to play with the cords, they were always getting wound around the mike stands, and seeing them being retrieved after I'd been out in a crowd was like watching a lifesaving team at work," Angus explained.

Following an eighteen-show jaunt to Europe in September and a fourteen-date British tour (including two sold-out shows at Hammersmith Odeon) the following month,

AC/DC returned to the U.S. in November for another six weeks of roadwork, headlining clubs while opening for the likes of KISS and Rush in arenas—where the scruffy shoestring road warriors would often have trouble convincing security personnel that they were actually a band. "We toured in a station wagon," Angus told *Guitar World*. "[KISS] had everything behind them, the media, a huge show and stuff. And here we were—five migrants, little micro people. It was tough to even get into the show with that station wagon. Many a time they wouldn't let us into the venue 'cause they didn't see a limo!"

The band's attack on the States had done much to raise AC/DC's stateside profile and led to *Let There Be Rock* cracking the lower reaches of the *Billboard* Top 200. Meanwhile, things were looking up in Britain as well, where the disc became the first AC/DC album to chart in the U.K., reaching a respectable if not earth-shattering number 75.

The band capped its American odyssey in December with a widely heard live radio broadcast from Atlantic's New York studios and a high-profile show with KISS at Madison Square Garden, before flying out to Sydney to record a new album.

The exhilaration of the successful U.S. tour was offset somewhat when the group's plans to tour during their stay in Australia were scuttled by, of all things, immigration problems. Ironically, because of AC/DC's new English bassist and predominantly British crew, Australian authorities refused to grant the visas necessary for AC/DC to perform in its country of origin.

"We used to think of ourselves as an Australian band, but we're beginning to doubt that now," Angus complained to *RAM*. "The fuckers won't even let us play here." It's hard to imagine a more blatant illustration of how far AC/DC had come from their Antipodean origins. In lieu of a tour, the band played a couple of semisecret shows at their old Sydney haunt the Lifesaver, billed as the Seedies. Perhaps as a result of AC/DC's failure to tour Australia, *Let There Be Rock* had ended up selling a relatively meager 25,000 copies there.

14

ROCK 'N' ROLL DAMNATION

AC/DC began 1978 in Sydney in the Albert studio with Vanda and Young, recording the album that would become *Powerage*. Despite the ignominy of being banned from touring in Australia, the album sessions were infused with an aura of positivity, thanks to the career strides that the band had made in the U.S., the U.K. and Europe. The band knew that its next album would have to be a hands-down winner, and *Powerage* did not disappoint.

The album's tongue-in-cheek front cover—depicting Angus, with a tangle of wires emerging from his sleeves, in the throes of a massive electrical shock—gave a good hint of the album's electrifying musical contents. "I suppose I look a bit like a Christmas tree," said Angus. "Plenty of balls, but without the fairy on top!"

Angus has claimed that half of *Powerage*'s tracks were recorded in a single take, and the songs' relentless energy made it easy to accept that claim. "Rock 'n' Roll Damnation"—which, at number 24, would become AC/DC's highest-charting British single to date—kicked off the album with a statement of purpose as powerful as anything the band had recorded. "Down Payment Blues" and "Gimme a Bullet" ably demonstrated the band's increasing focus, while "Sin City" and "Gone Shootin'" possessed a decidedly sinister edge. And Angus delivered some of his most bracing guitar work yet on "Riff Raff," "What's Next to the Moon," "Up to My Neck in You" and "Kicked in the Teeth."

Now in a position to consolidate the beginnings of international success into honest-to-goodness stardom, AC/DC hit the road with a vengeance. The *Powerage* world tour was launched at the end of April with twenty-eight U.K. dates, including a gig in Dundee, Scotland, that saw Angus sailing off the stage yet managing to avoid serious injury.

The *Powerage* tour was the most elaborate and prestigious that AC/DC had undertaken thus far, with a careful emphasis placed on such remunerative nonmusical areas as merchandising. More important, the shows featured an upgraded P.A. that allowed the full range of Bon Scott's singular instrument to be heard properly for the first time and added new resonance to Angus Young's rapidly evolving guitar sound. Speaking of new gear, the tour found the pint-sized axeman showing off a shiny new set of front teeth to replace the rotted choppers that had previously inhabited that provocative mouth.

From June through October, the band undertook a marathon seventy-six-date U.S. trek. In America they opened shows for the likes of Aerosmith, Alice Cooper and Journey, but found that their reputation as an incendiary live unit caused many big-name artists to fear sharing stages with them. At Chicago's Summer Jam, AC/DC upstaged the higher-billed likes of Aerosmith, Van Halen and Foreigner in front of an audience of forty thousand. In August, at New York's Palladium, they stole the show from their old nemesis Ritchie Blackmore when they opened for his Rainbow. A week and a half later, in their demographic stronghold of Jacksonville, Florida, AC/DC headlined over Cheap Trick and Molly Hatchet in front of a sellout crowd of fourteen thousand. From there, the quintet traveled to the West Coast, playing a series of dates with Aerosmith before headlining at L.A.'s Starwood.

Reviewing the Starwood gig for *Sounds,* Sylvie Simmons wrote, "There's something about this band that can get you moving quicker than milk of magnesia" and described the scene inside the auditorium as "a Ken Russell vision of rock 'n' roll hell," before concluding, "Why can't more rock 'n' roll bands be like this?"

Although they had little trouble outshining Aerosmith, who were then in the throes of the drug-induced slump that would eventually temporarily put the band out of commission, AC/DC was weathering some internal dilemmas of its own. While Bon had yet to be seriously debilitated by the effects of his immoderation, the rigors of the road were definitely beginning to take their toll on Phil Rudd.

Rudd, who was still doing much of the driving on the band's low-budget tours, had on several occasions suffered from exhaustion escalated by his use of drugs, to the point of having to be taken to local hospitals for sedation.

"I think touring is what you make of it," Angus told *Sounds,* rather dismissively. "I do get fidgety if we have a day off, because touring is geared around twiddling your thumbs and getting ready for the show. If the show's missing, the day just doesn't feel right."

During the *Powerage* tour, the band encountered more of the sort of incidents that would enhance its reputation as a magnet for on-the-road trouble. In Detroit the promoter pulled the plug on the band after five songs, complaining about excessive volume. According to band-propagated legend, the musicians waited patiently until after they'd been paid for their performance, and then Malcolm punched the promoter in the face. The promoter threatened to call the police, the band threatened to sue, and the incident ended in a stalemate.

By the year's end, *Powerage* had become AC/DC's first gold album, selling a quite respectable one hundred and fifty thousand copies. But as Bon told Melbourne's *Daily Herald,* success hadn't spoiled him. "All that has changed is my intake of alcohol. I can now afford to drink twice as much."

In October, just six months after *Powerage*'s release, fans got *If You Want Blood, You've Got It,* an appropriately sweaty live album recorded during the recent tour. From its playfully gruesome cover, which captured the sight of the onstage Angus impaled by his own guitar neck, to its rough-and-ready renditions of ten of the band's hottest live numbers (most of them drawn from *Let There Be Rock* and *Powerage*), the album offered an excellent representation of AC/DC's potency as a live act.

Coinciding with the live album's release, the band staged a ragingly successful lightning-raid tour of Britain, encompassing sixteen shows in eighteen days. It was during a stop at the Glasgow Apollo that Bon, prior to show time, stepped outside for a breath of fresh air and, not having a ticket or backstage pass in his possession, found himself refused readmittance to the venue.

"I went around front and they wouldn't let me in until I found a T-shirt vendor who attested to my identity," the vocalist recounted. "By that time, ten minutes had gone by, and everyone was saying, 'Where is that S.O.B.?' "

The band members' punishing, near-constant touring and

recording schedule left little time for personal lives. "None of us have had our own places to live for the past two years," Bon said. "I rented a flat for eight months but I was only there for six weeks. All we've got is our parents' homes in Australia. We live in hotels, and we don't say at the end of a gig, 'I'm goin' back to the hotel,' we've got into the habit of sayin', 'I'm goin' home.' "

"The band live like the Mafia," Angus concurred. "Bon's always been of no fixed abode and I'm in the flat above. If you're really wealthy, maybe you can afford to say, 'Whammo, I'll have that block of apartments there.' I suppose I'll buy a place sometime, but I'll probably end up with one of those police boxes at a city crossroads so I can be in the thick of it. At the moment I'm quite at home in these motels. I'll go to me parents at Christmas, and after a week I'll check into a hotel. I mean, I've got brothers who bring their kids round and at six in the mornin' they'll fuckin' jump on you yellin', 'He's home!' In a hotel I could complain about the noise and change rooms."

If You Want Blood's sales success offered further evidence of AC/DC's ascendant status. In Britain it rose to number 13 on the album charts, while in America it became the first AC/DC album to hit the Top 50. In Australia, where the band was still unable to tour, it wasn't released until Christmas, and its relatively lackluster sales once again reflected the group's continuing absence from the Australian touring circuit.

Once again, the band returned to Australia at Christmastime with the intention of recording a new album. In a December 9, 1978, interview with the *Melbourne Sun*, Bon looked forward to visiting with his parents in Perth. "I haven't seen them for three years," he said. "I hope they recognize me."

15

THIS MEANS WAR

Though returning to its country of origin to make a new record had by now become a yearly ritual, on this trip AC/DC's plans quickly went awry. While the band waited in Sydney for Atlantic's official go-ahead to begin recording, Michael Klenfner flew in to personally deliver the news that the company—which had long harbored reservations about George Young and Harry Vanda's minimalist production approach—now wanted AC/DC to record with a producer who could give the group a cleaner recorded sound that would help them attain the U.S. radio airplay that had long eluded them. Klenfner informed the band that the man the company had chosen for the job was on his way to Sydney to meet with the band.

George, who more than anyone was responsible for AC/DC's transition from raw pub band to recording act, publicly took his unceremonious deposal graciously, but privately he was furious. The official line, at least, was that the

Vanda/Young team agreed that it was time for an infusion of new blood.

"George said 'Go ahead,' " Angus claimed. "He told us, 'Don't let them mess with what you are. Always remember you're a rock 'n' roll band.' "

While in interviews the band downplayed the split with the producers that helped make them famous, Angus and Malcolm were apparently deeply torn between their ambition to succeed at all odds—an inclination that they had, to some degree, picked up from George—and their loyalty to their brother. But the bottom line, as the Youngs and Michael Browning understood, was that the band wasn't in much of a position to resist, and they reluctantly acceded to Atlantic's wishes.

The man that the company had chosen for the task of making AC/DC's sound palatable for U.S. radio consumption was Eddie Kramer, whose résumé included work with Jimi Hendrix and KISS. As if the prospect of recording without George and Harry wasn't traumatic enough, it quickly became clear that the match between the band and the fast-talking, New York–bred Kramer was manufactured somewhere other than heaven. Atlantic had flown Kramer to Australia to record a track with the group as a waters-testing trial, before sending band and producer to Miami to write and record the album, but the vibes steadily worsened until the situation could no longer be salvaged.

Frustrated with their fruitless attempts at putting together material with Kramer, whom they claimed had tried to get them to record a cover of the old Spencer Davis Group hit "Gimme Some Lovin' " in an attempt to score a surefire radio hit, the band took matters into their own hands. Malcolm put in an agitated phone call to Michael Browning, who was staying at the New York apartment of fellow manager Clive Calder, whose clients included producer Robert John "Mutt"

Lange. Lange happened to be present when Malcolm called, and Browning, who held Lange's talents in high regard, asked him to consider stepping in.

As Bon later told *RAM*, "Three weeks in Miami and we hadn't written a thing with Kramer. So one day we told him we were going to have the day off and not to bother coming in. We snuck into the studio and on that one day we put down six songs, sent the tape to Lange and said, 'Will you work with us?' " Lange was impressed by the new demos—written and recorded by Angus, Malcolm and Bon, with Bon doubling on drums—and the band headed for London to begin working with Lange on salvaging the increasingly frustrating project.

The South African–born Lange would seem to have been an unlikely candidate to produce AC/DC, as his experience was limited to less ear-shattering acts like Graham Parker and the Rumor, the Boomtown Rats and City Boy. But the band insisted on using Lange, standing firm against Michael Klenfner's objections. The decision would prove to be one of the best that the group ever made.

The band, which had not previously recorded outside of Australia and had never spent more than three weeks working on an album, spent nearly three months putting in fifteen-hour days with Lange at London's Roundhouse Studios, putting together the album that would become *Highway to Hell.*

"In the past we really never had much time to spend recording, because we were always on the road, so our albums tended to be very rushed," Angus commented upon the album's release in the summer of 1979. "Last year we spent ten months touring, and prior to that we hadn't had a break since the band began. We'd just go in and do the albums—which, of course, were mainly written on the road—and we never really had time to sit back and plan things."

Indeed, Lange, whose meticulous recording philosophy differed substantially from the Vanda/Young team's relatively low-fi garage approach, did an admirable job of refining and sharpening AC/DC's sound without losing the raw edge that was the source of the band's original appeal. "It was an experience for Lange, because he'd never worked with anyone as hard as us," Angus related, adding, "We benefited more than anything from his work with Bon."

Indeed, *Highway to Hell* saw Bon Scott benefiting from such heretofore untried recording techniques as double-tracking and backing vocals without sacrificing the band's edge, as evidenced by the subtle backing vocals of "Touch Too Much." "It's a bit different, it's melodic," Bon marveled. "They coaxed me into singing notes as opposed to screaming notes. And there's harmonies even. AC/DC singing harmonies!"

"I think the thing about *Highway to Hell* was that Mutt knew what FM stereo sounded like and we didn't," Angus told *Musician* magazine. "Every week he'd be there with the Top 10 of America, listening to the sounds. And he's got a great set of ears. He could hear a pin drop. I know Bon was very happy with him. Mutt taught Bon to breathe, bring it from your stomach. After we'd done the album, Bon said to Mutt, 'I like what you've done. Do you think it would be worth it for me to go off and learn with somebody?' Mutt said, 'No, I don't. This is you.' And I think Mutt learned something from us as well. I think he was impressed that we could play and knew what a song was, as opposed to just a riff."

"Mutt knew how we felt; he didn't go too far with us, which we liked," Malcolm told *RAM*. "We learnt a lot. We're used to having George to lean on. A lot of ideas we wouldn't finish because you'd wait to see what George might spark for us. This way we had to have all the ideas written, arranged. Then Mutt would do little bits. You really need an outsider, because we can all go too far and disappear up our own anuses." High praise indeed, coming from a member of a band whose suspicion of outsiders was the stuff of legend.

Whatever the emotional issues attached to the split with Vanda and Young, anyone who listened to *Highway to Hell* had to admit that the change in producers and recording methodology had resulted in AC/DC's strongest, most dynamic music to date. "This album is the best thing we've done," said Angus. "We ended up with enough songs for four albums. But we picked songs with new ideas."

"The bottom line," added Bon, "is still very much hard rock, but we've used more melody and backing vocals to enhance the sound. It's possible there is a more commercial structure to the music, without going the whole way. In the past, it's just been a total scream, so I worked on it a lot more this time."

Whatever the band's reservations about dumping George and Harry, no one could dispute the fact that Lange had accomplished what the ousted production team hadn't, giving AC/DC a sound hard-hitting enough to please its die-hard fans yet with sufficient focus to give the band a shot at scoring some much-needed U.S. airplay.

Highway to Hell was a landmark album, not only for AC/DC but for the hard-rock genre in general, boasting a fuller, more lively sound utilizing the potential of contemporary studio hardware without sacrificing the music's essential simplicity. The title track is one of rock's great anthems, a self-mocking paean to the lure of the rock lifestyle, while numbers like "Girls Got Rhythm," "Walk All Over You," "Beating Around the Bush," "Shot Down in Flames" and "Get It Hot" were perfect showcases for the album's more sophisticated recording approach. And "If You Want Blood (You've Got It)" continued in the *High Voltage* tradition of AC/DC album titles popping up later as song titles.

The album-closing "Night Prowler" would a few years later become a source of nonmusical frustration for the band, but at the time, it was simply a song that had been kicking around in various forms for a while. "We had that title two years ago and we've recorded four different versions, but this time around a new idea came out that made it work," said Angus. "That often happens—you have the right title and idea for the song but can't find the right package. And there's no point in wasting a good idea on a bum song."

Just about the only one of the album's ten tracks that didn't become a virtual standard was "Love Hungry Man," the only *Highway to Hell* number that didn't find a place in AC/DC's live sets. "The overall thing was a lot rougher on our original demos," explained Malcolm. "In the studio it didn't happen right. But we had to settle for it. But it doesn't mean the band have to like it or listen to it."

16

THIS HOUSE IS ON FIRE

Highway to Hell marked a turning point for AC/DC, musically and otherwise. To no one's surprise, the album—released on July 27, 1979—became AC/DC's first U.S. million-seller as well as its first entry in the American Top 20, not to mention the band's first British Top 10 album. It was even a hit in Australia, where it made it to number 24, making it the first AC/DC album to chart there in nearly three years.

The music's focused aggression made it clear that the extra time and effort in the studio had been worthwhile. With Mutt Lange's production finally adding the final piece of the puzzle, the band was clearly ready to take its place at the top of the heap.

According to some observers, though, the ill feelings stirred up by the sacking of George and Harry helped to intensify the band's traditional insularity. One result of this ongoing state of affairs was to increase Bon Scott's growing sense of alienation from his bandmates. The situation also had an adverse effect on the Young brothers' rapport with Michael Browning, who served as a convenient scapegoat for their own feelings of guilt over George's dismissal.

Further, the Albert organization and Browning's office were both financially overextended, due to the enormous costs of mounting the band's various international campaigns. Word of the situation began to filter through the music-industry grapevine, and various American management entities began sniffing around, in hopes of grabbing a piece of the action.

Meanwhile, an effort by Browning to bring New York promoter Cedric Kushner into the picture as a partner/investor backfired when Kushner's questioning of the band's contracts with the Albert office aroused Angus and Malcolm's fortress-mentality tendencies, contributing to an increasing atmosphere of distrust, which ultimately led to Browning's dismissal. As with so many former band members and business associates before him, Browning was gradually phased out of official accounts of AC/DC's history.

Waiting in the wings was Peter Mensch of the powerful New York–based Leber and Krebs organization, which since its formation in 1972 had established itself as one of the rock business's shrewdest and most aggressive management firms. In 1979, though, Leber-Krebs was in a bit of a slump due to the flagging fortunes of its two best-known clients, Aerosmith and Ted Nugent. The combination of the rising but cash-poor AC/DC and the slightly faded but still-powerful Leber-Krebs was an inspired match. The band would get the funding and connections that its new management could provide, while the firm would benefit from the prestige of a hot young act.

Business shake-ups aside, on a purely musical level AC/DC had never been stronger. *Highway to Hell* received the most positive press of the band's career. Even *New Musical Express* stated, "By taking all the unfashionable clichés and metaphors of heavy rock, discarding every ounce of the genre's attendant flab, and fusing those ingredients with gall, simplicity and deceptive facility into a dynamic whole, they have created an aesthetic of their own."

The band, whose touring entourage had by now swelled to about twenty-five, spent the remainder of 1979 touring behind *Highway to Hell* in the U.S. and Britain, though still not in Australia, where the album wasn't released until October. At this point, the live show featured "Live Wire" (the band's standard opening number), "The Jack," "High Voltage" and "Rocker" from the Australian *TNT;* "Let There Be Rock," "Bad Boy Boogie," "Problem Child" and "Hell Ain't a Bad Place to Be" from *Let There Be Rock;* and "Riff Raff" and "Sin City" from *Powerage,* along with the bulk of *Highway to Hell.* The encore of choice was "Whole Lotta Rosie."

In the States AC/DC played a handful of headlining shows while opening other concerts for the likes of Cheap Trick, UFO and Leber-Krebs stablemate Ted Nugent, who, ironically, had dubbed his tour "TNT." The band also played such high-profile festival gigs as San Francisco's Day and Cheap Trick's Independence Day bash in Rockford, Illinois.

For AC/DC's last show as Cheap Trick's opening act, Angus, Malcolm and Bon bounded onstage for the headliners' encore, which included renditions of AC/DC's "Sin City" and Chuck Berry's "School Day" (previously a staple of early AC/DC's club gigs). The encore also found Cheap Trick guitarist Rick Nielsen being hoisted on the shoulders of a roadie à la Angus.

But not all headliners regarded the idea of sharing the stage with AC/DC with such enthusiasm. In fact, the band's reputation as a take-no-prisoners performing unit was making it increasingly difficult to find big-name bands willing to follow them. In attempting to book the U.S. *Highway to Hell* tour, AC/DC was turned down by Foreigner, Van Halen and Sammy Hagar. "Our aim," Bon gloated, "is to make the headliners work for their money."

On July 30 an open-air show in Cleveland, on which AC/DC shared a bill with Ted Nugent, Aerosmith, Journey and Thin Lizzy, erupted into a riot when a gunman let loose on the sixty-thousand-strong crowd. One fan was shot to death, another seriously wounded, and over three hundred police officers were called in to quell the resulting panic.

Despite working extensively in the United States, Angus still expressed reservations about America. "I'm happy playing; when I go onstage, I'm happy. America . . . I don't like the TV and things like that, the food I don't like, it's all fake . . . And I don't like every time you turn on the TV there's some guy running for president."

The British leg of the *Highway to Hell* tour took in dates in Newcastle, Glasgow, Liverpool, Stafford and London's Hammersmith Odeon, with support act Def Leppard in tow. On August 18, AC/DC opened for the Who at London's Wembley arena, a show that marked the headliners' grand return after a three-year hiatus from live performance and its first London show with new drummer Kenney Jones. AC/DC rose to the occasion and played a particularly impressive set, at least until halfway through "Whole Lotta Rosie," when the P.A. went out—unbeknownst to the band, who could still hear themselves in their amps and monitors and carried on playing. Despite the sound problems, AC/DC's set won excellent notices and was undoubtedly helpful in expanding the group's audience.

Angus and Malcolm were particularly honored that AC/DC was on the bill at the headliners' request, since the Who was one of the few bands that they would admit to admiring. Indeed, Pete Townshend is virtually the only guitarist that Angus will admit to being influenced by. "I've not been influenced much by other guitarists," he maintains. "So far as listening goes I've always got off more on other instruments than the guitar. Things like saxophones and clarinets—they wail better. They don't just put their left foot forward, they get to the heart of the matter and sink their teeth in. I don't really listen to a lot of other music, but in terms of rock, I like Townshend—I saw him, and every time he swung his arms, he did hit his guitar!"

The Wembley gig did a lot for AC/DC's credibility and confidence, and led to more outdoor dates with the Who in Europe. Reviewing the Wembley show, Australia's *Juke* captured a good deal of the band's appeal: "AC/DC are not 'good' or 'bad.' They are perfect AC/DC, a heavy metal archetype overblown to the point where stereotype meets parody. Is Bon Scott serious or what? Is he just playing out a real-life comic strip of an HM lead singer? Do they smirk when they write those giant three-chord riffs? Or do they just know that the world will love something this crass?"

Reviewing the group's Hammersmith Odeon gig, a portion of which was broadcast by the BBC as part of its *In Concert* series, the *NME*'s Stuart Johnson struck a similar note of condescension. "The music was ugly, and . . . the almost exclusively male audience was the ugliest I've seen outside of a Glasgow Rangers game. . . . Do they like the music because they're ugly or do they become ugly as a result of it? . . . What this music has to do with rock 'n' roll is no longer even a question worth asking. It's clearly a sub-culture of its own and its devotees neither want nor deserve any better."

By the time AC/DC got back to America, it was greeted by a fan base that had obviously grown in numbers and enthusiasm, indicating that the work the band had put in was paying off. Now they were headlining in the States over such acts as Pat Travers and Molly Hatchet and beginning to get airplay even on America's more conservative album-rock stations. The live show was still as basic and unadorned as ever, the visual hooks provided by Angus's and Bon's wacky stage personae.

As *Sounds'* Sylvie Simmons, reviewing an October AC/DC gig in Long Beach, California, confessed, "I'm drawn to this depraved quintet simply because they're here once again, and because amid this ever-changing universe they can be relied on to be much the same as last time."

By the time of the *Highway to Hell* tour, Angus's striptease routine had become such a familiar ritual that he sometimes received help from overenthusiastic audience members. One night, he explained, "The kids pulled my pants off—a bit embarrassing, but it does make you popular." At another show, "Someone ripped off my sneakers. I was rolling around on the floor onstage and some kid in the front row dived over and pinched them. I put up a good fight trying to get them back, but between him and his friends there wasn't much left except one-inch pieces!"

At a show at Long Island's Calderone Concert Hall, an audience member tossed a drink at Angus, to which the ever-feisty axeman responded by throwing down his guitar and diving into the audience to knock some sense into the perpetrator. "I had a bit of a punch up that night," he told *Circus.* "I got the fright of my life. The guy had been spitting on me and throwing things and giving me a hard time. And Mal doesn't like me disrupting [the show]. His big advice to me was, 'Just ignore it, Ang.' But that night I just had enough. So I put the guitar down and I went for him. The trouble was, when I hit him he kept going."

Bon presented the band with yet another first-rate example

of his knack for attracting trouble after a refueling stop at a Phoenix airport en route to a show in Austin, Texas. When the plane took off again, the rest of the band noticed that their singer was missing. Apparently, he'd struck up a friendship with a woman on the plane and followed her off when they landed in Phoenix.

Bon's version of the story went like this: "We'd been drinking in the airport bar for about ten minutes when I says, 'Don't you think it's time we caught our plane?' and she says, 'What do you mean our plane? I'm staying here.' I runs back and the fuckin' flight's gone. Anyway she takes me to this black bar—she was Mexican—and I starts drinkin' and playin' pool. I had a good night, beatin' every bastard. After about two hours playin' this big-titted black chick and beatin' her too, I happen to look and the whole bar is goin' 'Grrr.' I think, 'Uh-oh Bon,' gives her another game and lose nine to one. 'Anyone else want to beat me?' I says. So I escapes with me life, only barely—and I made it to the gig in Austin."

Though his bandmates shared an ability to pace themselves while on tour, the famously immoderate Bon continued to deal with the rigors of the road through drink and debauchery. Though he was a reliable pro who rarely missed a gig, Scott's offstage pastimes of drinking and womanizing, along with his increasing use of pills, were a growing source source of worry for those around him.

After a show in San Antonio, Texas, the band's backstage revelry was briefly interrupted when Bon accidentally swallowed a bottle of aftershave lotion. And after overimbibing at a party thrown by Atlantic prior to the first of the band's 1979 sellout gigs at Hammersmith Odeon, Scott had to have his stomach pumped before he could perform. It was obvious that the singer's offstage pursuits were posing a significant threat to his health.

While both Angus and Malcolm were involved in long-term relationships with women they would later marry, thinking about settling down and buying houses, Bon continued his wandering ways, insisting that he wasn't yet ready to settle down, continuing to seek his redemption in alcohol, womanizing and rock 'n' roll.

According to English road manager Ian Jeffery, who'd been with the band since 1976, "When we're headlining, we've got twenty-five people on the road. One semitrailer packed with lights and rigging, two more with sound equipment and staging. Two buses for the band and the crew to mount this size show . . . With a big production in medium-sized halls you have to pack the halls. You make enough money on the tour so you don't have to get support from the record company. This tour should just break even. You hope all those people go and buy the record so the next time around you can move to bigger halls and make some money."

The band's preferred method of transport was bus rather than plane. "With the bus you can leave at midday and still arrive late afternoon," Cliff Williams pointed out. "Or you can drive all night after a gig and sleep the next day. But planes fly early or late, and you've got to get to and from the airport, you lose your bags—it's a pain in the arse."

On the way to Australia for the by-now-traditional Christmas visit (which once again would not involve the recording of a new LP), AC/DC stopped off in Europe for a series of dates, including a one-off Paris concert with Judas Priest; the band's set was filmed and would eventually emerge as the concert movie *Let There Be Rock*. It had now been three years since AC/DC had toured Australia; with *Highway to Hell* reestablishing the band's commercial stock in its homeland, the band was keen to play there again. But the expense involved in transporting the band's entourage and stage gear to

Australia could only be justified if dates in Japan could be lined up to make a trip to the Eastern Hemisphere financially viable. They weren't. Bon Scott would never grace a stage in his homeland again.

On the road, Bon carried a tape recorder, on which he'd record bits of lyrical inspiration for future reference; he once claimed that he'd play the tapes for his mother and keep the lyrics that offended her the most. On the *Highway to Hell* tour the tape recorder was stolen. As Angus later explained, "One night Bon got drunk. Three months later he sobered up and it was gone."

17

KICKED IN THE TEETH

AC/DC spent January 1980 tying up loose ends and preparing to begin work on the all-important follow-up to *Highway to Hell.* The band flew to France for an appearance at the annual Midem music-industry convention, at which they were presented with an armload of gold and silver discs for sales in France and Canada. They also played make-up dates in Newcastle and Southampton for shows canceled on the last U.K. tour and taped an appearance on British TV's *Top of the Pops* to promote the current U.K. single "Touch Too Much." Angus, meanwhile, was making plans for his wedding to his Dutch fiancée, Ellen.

Bon moved into new digs in London's Victoria district, where he continued to work on writing lyrics for the new LP. Despite his various indulgences, the singer seemed to be in good spirits, and enthusiastic about the upcoming album project. But some of Bon's friends had detected subtle changes in his usually happy-go-lucky exterior, and some noted an apparent deterioration in his physical health. He had also confided to friends his growing frustration with AC/DC's narrow stylistic parameters, expressing a desire to record a solo album that would allow him to explore more personal influences that he couldn't address in his work with the band.

On the night of February 20, Bon had been drinking with a musician friend named Alistair Kinnear at a club called the Music Machine in London's Camden Town. The pair left the club at 3:00 A.M., by which time Bon had reportedly consumed seven double whiskeys—certainly a substantial amount, though not especially remarkable by Scott's prodigious standards of consumption. After driving home to Scott's flat, Kinnear was unable to rouse Bon, who had fallen unconscious. After arriving at his own home, Kinnear was still unable to awaken his passenger, so he wrapped some blankets around Scott and left him in the car to sleep it off. After sleeping for about fifteen hours, Kinnear woke and checked Bon at about 7:45 on the evening of the twenty-first, and discovered that Scott was dead. The singer was pronounced dead on arrival at London's Kings College Hospital.

The hospital called Bon's girlfriend, Silver Smith, whose name Kinnear had given as Scott's next of kin. She called Angus Young, who called the hospital, who would not discuss Scott's status over the phone because he was not a family member. Angus then phoned Peter Mensch, who went to the hospital with Ian Jeffery and confirmed that Bon was indeed dead. "Peter got to the hospital as soon as he could," said Angus, "to find out exactly what had happened and identify him, because everyone was in doubt at the time. At first, I didn't really believe it, but in the morning it finally dawned on me . . . Malcolm rang Bon's parents 'cause we didn't want them to be just sitting there and suddenly it comes on the TV news, you know."

An initial report recorded the cause of death as acute alcohol poisoning, but it was later determined that Scott had moved in his sleep, vomited and choked to death. At a coroner's inquest, at which the singer's bandmates offered testimony, the coroner reported that Scott's stomach had contained the "equivalent of half a bottle of whiskey" when he died and officially designated Bon's demise as death by misadventure.

Bon was cremated and buried in a quiet funeral service on March 1 in his old stamping grounds of Fremantle, Australia. One of the reasons it was so quiet was that many of Bon's friends were not informed of the funeral. The Albert office's protectiveness had the added effect of keeping the media away, simply because they never found out about the service. "The funeral itself was more or less quiet, though there were a lot of kids outside," said Angus. "It was better being quiet, because it could have been very bad if a lot of people had just converged there."

In a press release issued by Atlantic, the singer was eulogized thusly: "Bon Scott was always the top joker in the AC/DC pack. The stories of his sexual and alcoholic excesses are legion and that part of his enormous fan mail that didn't involve tempting offers from young girl fans invariably berated him for 'leading poor Angus astray.' Sadly, Bon is no longer with us after he tragically went just one step too far on one of his notorious boozing binges. But if there is a crumb of comfort to be found in such a needless and premature death, it is that Bon probably went out the way that he would have chosen, never flinching as he went over the top just one more time."

Atlantic's copywriter was apparently unfamiliar with the concept that alcoholism is a disease, not an antiestablishment stance. A far more eloquent tribute came from Angus himself in an exhaustive interview with the English music weekly *Sounds:* "Bon was like a father to us all. He was about ten years older than I was and he had all the experience and knowledge. If there was a problem with getting paid after a show, Bon was the one who handled it. If we had a personal problem, Bon was the one we went to. He was a very special person . . . He was one of a kind.

"Often Bon would trail off with fans who came backstage after a show and go off with them to a party or elsewhere. He judged people as they were and if they invited him somewhere and he was in the right mood to go, he went. It didn't matter to him whether they had a name or were a 'star,' he just went with them. We used to call him 'Bon the Likeable.'

Angus expressed sympathy for Alistair Kinnear, opining that "he thought he was doing the right thing at the time, 'cause he'd been out with Bon a few times, and Bon had done the same thing before. I've seen Bon on many occasions drink three bottles of bourbon straight off, and he could drink like that constantly. He was basically healthy; it was just the position he was in the car that did it . . . I've seen Bon fall asleep behind amplifiers. One moment he could be sitting watching TV and the next he would stand up, walk behind a couch and, bonk, fall over asleep. He was just like that; when he had a drink he could sleep anywhere, but he'd always be fine when he woke up in the morning. He would be up to three or four in the morning drinking his heart out, and then up again about ten the next day to get a plane, and he was always a picture of health. He was remarkable.

"The thing is, the last two years of his life was probably the most sober I saw him," Angus later claimed in a *Musician* interview. "He just had a magnet for a party. 'Anything I do, you don't do,' he used to tell me when I'd tag along for the night. AC/DC was his life, like it is for me. So it was like losing family, 'cause we probably saw more of each other. He had come out of bands that wanted him to sing like someone else. We wanted him to sing like him.

"It was just like losing a member of our own family, maybe even worse, because we all had a lot of respect for Bon as a person, 'cause, even though he did like to drink and have a bit of a crazy time, he was always there when you needed him to do his job, and I think in his whole career there's maybe only three shows he ever missed, and that was 'cause his voice wasn't there and we didn't really want him to sing. But I think it's more sad for the guy himself, you know, 'cause he always said he would never go unless he was famous.

"Malcolm and I were really looking forward to getting Bon in the studio," Angus said at the time, "more than we'd done with any album before, because, after the success of the last one it was going to be a really big challenge, you know. That was the saddest part of it, 'cause it could perhaps have been the best thing he'd ever done on record. I think that's the real loss for everyone, especially the fans, 'cause they would've had a chance to hear him at his peak. That would have been the crowning glory of his life."

Despite his personal excesses, Bon Scott's rebellion wasn't nihilistic or antisocial. Indeed, he had always maintained a loving and respectful relationship with his parents and was unfailingly considerate with friends and fans alike. But for his entire adult life, he built a lifestyle around his rejection of the conformity of the dreary, emotionally repressive class system he'd been raised in, and his all-encompassing personal rebellion was reflected in both his writing and his singing. Rock 'n' roll gave him a new sense of purpose, of belonging. His colorful exploits aside, it's nigh on impossible to find anyone with a bad word to say about Scott. Those who knew him remember his generosity and professionalism rather than his indulgences.

Scott's contribution to AC/DC cannot be underestimated. He brought a genuine inventiveness and skill to his work, even if the simplicity of his art was often mistaken for shallowness. His lyrics were not merely random dirty jokes strung together, but compelling stories, abounding with experience, drawn from his years in the streets and on the road.

When Bon joined AC/DC, Angus and Malcolm, for all their bravado, were green and relatively inexperienced in the ways of the rock world. Bon was the living embodiment of their rock 'n' roll ideal, and his professional know-how and stage presence gave AC/DC a fresh new dimension that made it possible for the band to realize its potential. And the evidence in the grooves of *Highway to Hell* made it clear that he was just beginning to hit his stride.

Bon was nothing if not true to his artistic vision, living for the moment and letting the chips fall where they may. Whatever one thinks of his reckless disregard for his own health and the effect his actions ultimately had on those who cared about him, it's undeniable that Bon Scott was The Real Thing.

It's dangerous, however, to romanticize the singer's problems. As Robert Ellis, an English photographer who'd been taken into AC/DC's confidence, wrote, Bon "was a real danger to himself and needed nearly constant minding . . . But he was nearly always the first down in the lobby (in the) morning, spruced up and ready to go. I warned him and anyone within earshot of the impending danger, but no one took any notice, least of all him."

As veteran Australian rock journalist Glenn A. Baker observed after Bon's death, "I encountered Bon Scott a number of times during the '70s, and each meeting served to increase my incredulity that a performer's public image could be so at odds with his real personality. Bon really was a sweet man. He was warm, friendly and uncommonly funny. He did not breathe fire, pluck wings off flies or eat children whole. And while his daunting stage persona was by no means fraudulent, it was most certainly a professional cloak that could be worn at convenient moments."

In death, Scott's status as an icon has only grown. His spirit has continued to loom large in the AC/DC mythos, regularly invoked as the embodiment of the humor, energy and lack of pretension inherent in AC/DC's music.

"He made a lot of friends everywhere and was always in contact with them, too," Angus said of Bon. "Weeks before Christmas he would have piles of cards and things, and he always wrote to everyone he knew, keeping them informed. Even his enemies, I think."

Within days of Bon Scott's funeral, a curious and oddly appropriate thing happened. Friends of Bon around the world started receiving Christmas cards from the dead rocker. Seems they had been delayed because he'd neglected to put sufficient postage on them. It was a fitting farewell from a guy who knew how to make a flashy exit.

18
BACK IN BUSINESS

Despite the shock of Scott's unexpected loss, it didn't take long for the Young brothers to determine that AC/DC's only option was to recruit a new frontman and forge ahead. It was appropriate that Malcolm, the band's original motivator, was the first to voice a desire to keep the band together, calling Angus two days after the funeral to suggest that the surviving members get together to rehearse.

"We didn't really know what to do during the first few weeks after Bon's [death]," said Angus. "It was as if we'd come so far and suddenly then what? But eventually Malcolm said that he and I were still writing and that we should really continue with it. There were a lot of commitments as well, a lot of people were dependent on us, so it seemed clear that we had to keep going."

"I thought, 'Well, fuck this, I'm not gonna sit around mopin' all fuckin' year,' " affirmed Malcolm. "So I just rang up Angus and aid, 'Do you wanna come back and rehearse?"

"It's probably a lot better to keep working rather than just say 'stop,' " Angus reasoned, "because then it becomes a lot harder and all you can do is think about something like that. So as soon as Malcolm and I came back from the funeral, we got straight back to work on the songs we'd been writing at the time it happened."

On a practical level, the likelihood of Angus and Malcolm breaking up AC/DC was rather slim. For one thing, *Highway to Hell*'s success represented the fulfillment of all of their hard work and ambition, and they weren't the type to let something as trivial as death stand in their way. For another, AC/DC had grown into a business organization involving considerably more than the four surviving band members. The financial interests of Leber-Krebs, the Albert organization and Atlantic Records were all riding on the band's ability to fulfill its commercial potential and justify those parties' investments of money, time and energy. The machine was in full swing, and one monkey—not even Bon Scott—wasn't going to stop this show.

Less than a month after Bon's death, Angus took time out from auditioning singers at a London rehearsal studio to give an exhaustive interview with *Sounds,* in which he insisted, "The band will have to carry on now 'cause there's a lot of commitment for us. There's been no pressure put on us to keep going or anything, but as a band we decided to do it, though it's pretty hard at the moment to say what direction or whatever we'll take 'cause with Bon it was a unique thing. He is a unique character, and we wouldn't like to have someone there who was a Bon imitator. It would be better to get someone who's a bit unique in their own way. The band's music will probably stay the same, but the vocals will be a bit different.

"We've already seen quite a few people," Angus reported, "but it's a very hard thing, 'cause there's so many people with good voices, you know, and we're looking for something a little bit different. It's hard to put a guy on the spot and say 'Right, sing!' and expect him to be at his best, you know. We've just brought maybe one guy down here a night . . . It's difficult for any guy to walk in knowing that Bon's just died and probably thinking we're all going to be a bit funny about a new guy singing his songs. In fact, if someone walked in tomorrow and clicked, then we'd go straight in and record it 'cause we've basically got all the songs and ideas—it just needs that one missing ingredient."

There was much speculation in the Australian media that the group's new frontman would be ex-Easybeats singer Stevie Wright, who since the Easybeats' 1970 breakup had recorded two solo albums under the Vanda/Young production team and beaten a debilitating heroin problem. By 1980 Wright was working as a drug counselor for the Sydney branch of the Salvation Army.

Actually, for quite a while the inside track belonged to young Australian singer Allan Fryer, then fronting an obscure Adelaide band called Fat Lip. Fryer, who was reportedly George Young's choice, was at one point actually informally told that the job was his. Ironically, Fryer would go on to front the hard-rock band Heaven, which included deposed AC/DC bassist Mark Evans and whose affairs were overseen by ousted AC/DC manager Michael Browning.

The circumstances of how AC/DC discovered Bon Scott's actual replacement—or at least the possibly apocryphal version that the band likes to tell—have since become a cornerstone of AC/DC lore. According to legend, a fan in Chicago, reading of the band's difficulties finding a suitable replacement, sent Leber-Krebs's New York office a tape of an album by the English glam-rock band Geordie, whose gravel-voiced vocalist, Brian Johnson, the fan felt might be a good candidate for the job. The tape was passed along to the band, which was so impressed by Johnson's lungpower that it immediately set out to track him down and ask if he was interested in auditioning for the job.

As it happened, Johnson was in his hometown of Newcastle, England, having more or less given up on his rock 'n' roll dreams. "I got this call from the band saying come down and look us over," he later recalled. "I said, 'Listen, I can't spare much time, can we make it quick?' I did what they wanted and went back home and didn't think any more about it, and then I heard I got the job."

Brian Johnson was born on October 5, 1948, in the gray, gloomy industrial city of Newcastle, in the north of England (not far from Scotland, in fact). Brian was the son of Alan Johnson, a sergeant major in the British army who'd done battle with Nazi Field Marshal Rommel's tanks in the desert during World War II, and his Italian war bride, Esther. As a child, Brian had acted in local television productions, but got the music bug in his early teens. He quit school in his mid-teens (like Angus, Malcolm and Bon) and began an apprenticeship as an industrial fitter in a local turbine factory, while spending his evenings singing with local bands. It wasn't until 1972, nearly a decade later, that he quit his day job and became a full-time performer with Geordie, which actually enjoyed a brief period of success in Britain, scoring three British Top 20 singles.

But Geordie's success was short-lived. Like Fraternity and AC/DC, Geordie left its hometown for London, where the band lived in poverty. "We used to get up at 5:00 in the morning and follow the milkman around," Brian later told *Musi-*

Brian goes for the gusto.
(Gary Gershoff, Retna)

cian. "We used to look in the window at Indian restaurants and wait for people to leave a half-eaten meal just so we could run in and steal it. Jesus, the things we'd do. We never saw a penny from the records."

As Geordie continued to struggle onward, with ever-diminishing results, Johnson grew increasingly frustrated. "I was disillusioned with the rock business. We were beginning to slog away at nothing . . . We used to buy music papers and see all these two-penny groups with stupid names getting wined and dined, while bands from the Northeast got ignored.

"I gave it up in about '75 because it was all wrong," he relates. "So I left and I didn't think I'd join a professional band again. Ever."

By 1980 Johnson was back in Newcastle, playing small-scale local gigs at night with a reconstituted Geordie while concentrating on his new vinyl car-roofing business by day. "Then the telephone call came through from this guy who I couldn't even remember hardly, and he said, 'There's a band that wants a singer and I can't tell you who it is.' And I said, 'I don't want to know if you can't tell it.' And he said, 'Well, I can tell you the initials,' so he told me, and I said that's strange, because the singer just died two weeks ago. And he said, 'They're really hardworking guys, you know. Nothing will stop them.' And I said, 'I've lost it, really, I've not sung professionally for four or five years or something.' I couldn't go down for about thirteen days because I had gigs with the local band. And I didn't want to make the lads lose money because I was going to an audition."

Johnson drove down to London, did the audition and was back in Newcastle the same day, in time to play a gig with Geordie. "I was dead nervous because I had never been to an audition in my life. I didn't know what to do. And they said,

'Well, what do you want to sing?' And I said, 'Well, we'll do something that we all know.' So we did one."

"We knew it would be very hard to find someone, but when Brian walked through the door, everyone was happy," said Angus. "He more or less fitted in straightaway. The thing was, we wanted to find someone who was a character, and that's exactly what he is."

A couple of days later, Brian was called back to London— for another audition, he thought. When he arrived, he was informed that he was AC/DC's new singer and that he had two weeks to come up with the lyrics for the band's next album. This was in late March, less than six weeks after Scott's death and a scant four weeks after his funeral.

As Brian recalled, "You know the first thing Angus and Malcolm said to me when I joined the band? They said, 'Do you mind if your feelings ever get hurt?' and I said 'Why?' They said, " 'Cause if you're going to join this band, you're going to be expected to take fucking stick. Because we've always been slagged off by every fucking reporter since we left Australia.' And I said, 'Well, I'm going to have to take stick anyway, taking Bon's place.' "

Brian did, however, find it tough to leave his friends in Geordie. "They made it so much easier for me, because they came to me and said, 'Don't pass up an opportunity like this, we'll manage.' " According to Johnson, AC/DC even paid Johnson's bandmates to compensate for the lack of income resulting from his departure.

The term "Geordie" was northern English slang for the sort of rugged, hardworking (and generally hard-drinking) man that Newcastle tended to produce, and the garrulous, good-natured Johnson—with his trademark cap and ripped jeans— certainly fit that archetype. "I'm a Newcastle lad through and through, and I still want it to be my home," he remarked shortly after joining AC/DC.

Asked to name his vocal influences, Johnson cited Ray Charles, Joe Cocker, Tina Turner, Jerry Lee Lewis, Howlin' Wolf and fellow Newcastle native Eric Burdon, whose brooding work with the Animals made that group one of the British Invasion's toughest bands. But, like his new bandmates, Johnson seemed blissfully unconcerned with most contemporary music. "I'm busy trying to get meself right, I don't have time to listen to anybody else."

Another thing Brian shared with Angus and Malcolm was a marked distrust of punk rock—which, after all, had helped put Geordie out of business. "Heavy metal has come back because it's honest, good-time music," commented Johnson. "Punk and all that was just an image that ripped people off. Johnny Rotten's a wanker, and that's all there is to it."

Brian had actually shared a bill with Bon Scott's old band Fraternity during its London days. Angus had said that Bon had spoken highly of Johnson's vocal and performing talents. "They supported Geordie in 1973 or '74. I remember going for a drink with him, but I cannot remember talking to him," Brian later commented. "He looked so different; I didn't know it was him in AC/DC."

Though he had never seen an AC/DC show and was only familiar with the band by reputation, Johnson realized that he had big shoes to fill, as he made clear in an interview with BBC DJ Tommy Vance. "I think Bon Scott had a bit of genius," the singer said admiringly. "It annoys me that nobody recognized that before. He used to sing great words, write great words. He had a little twist in everything he said. Nobody ever recognized the man at the time. Oh great, when the man died they were startin' to say, 'Yeah, the man was a genius.' That was too late; it's not fair. I think he was so clever, and I think he had such a distinctive voice as well. He was brilliant."

Johnson's levelheadedness and friendly, easygoing manner eased his entry into the band on a social level, and his energy and hands-on know-how made him an asset on stage and in the studio. From the start, the band seemed confident that they'd made the right choice. "Yes, there were people who could imitate Bon, but I knew we wouldn't go for someone like that," said Angus. "Obviously we wanted someone to match Bon's capabilities but we didn't want a carbon copy.

"You've got to remember he's in a hard position," Angus observed. "Every night onstage, people are going to be looking at him and judging him until we've played every town we've ever been to in the past. They'll all be looking at him saying, 'That's the new guy, eh?' He's on the spot, and so he's got to push himself forward. Brian's one of those people who tries extremely hard, and when he sings he actually believes in what he's singing."

Johnson, meanwhile, felt a deeply rooted need to prove himself, and not only to AC/DC fans. "For ten years I've not only had the burden of carrying me wife and family, but also having people saying all the time that I've been wrong. So it's nice at the end of the day to turn around and say, 'Well, I might be a little bit late, I'm not exactly an overnight sensation, but . . .'"

19

RISING POWER

With Johnson on board, the band needed to move quickly to write and record their next album, which had fallen behind schedule due to Scott's death. With Johnson providing lyrics for the music that Angus and Malcolm had already written, the newly outfitted AC/DC spent the first half of April 1980 in London, rehearsing rigorously with Mutt Lange in hurried preparation for recording. In deference to Britain's restrictive tax codes, the sessions took place in the rather un–rock 'n' roll environs of Compass Point Studios in Nassau, Bahamas, through the end of May.

"There were a lot of different reasons for us finally deciding to work out there," Angus claimed. "Tax was one of them, and another was the actual availability of studios. We wanted somewhere in England because the country has a great working atmosphere. We didn't really want to go over to Europe since most of the stuff from there tends to be disco. There was one in Sweden that Zeppelin used, but that belongs to ABBA, and at that point they themselves were using it. But we didn't want to hang around waiting, we just wanted to get on with it.

"It's actually very slow at Compass Point," he continued. "I mean, the studio itself is very good, but the lifestyle is such that you tend to spend half the day lying around on the beach and having to work at night. But we didn't do that. Once we start working we want to get on with it."

Still, newcomer Johnson felt particularly out of place in his new tropical milieu. "I was plucked out of the working-class environment of Newcastle and suddenly chucked into the Bahamas, with all this sand and sun and palm trees," he mused. "I didn't like it, and the lads hated it as well. And trying to do a rock 'n' roll album there . . .

"Plus the fact that half the songs were half-written, [and I'm] sitting there thinking, 'Is this gonna work out right? If it doesn't work out right, I'm gonna be the biggest scapegoat the world's ever known.' If it didn't work out well, they could have just said, 'That was a waste of time,' and thrown it in the bin and said, 'Let's try it with someone else.' That was all running through me mind, because I didn't realize what I had taken on . . . I was so relieved at the end, when the first phone call came through from the manager saying, 'Oh, great, brilliant.' And Atlantic phoned up and said, 'Fantastic, it's gonna do the business.' For three days when I came back from the Bahamas, I just sat in the chair at home and didn't move."

But *Back in Black,* Johnson's AC/DC debut, made it abundantly clear that the singer had nothing to worry about. His gravelly howl, rougher and higher-pitched than Bon Scott's but no less gutsy, perfectly complemented the band's sound, echoing his predecessor's raw power while remaining completely individual.

The new album's title, along with its all-black cover, tastefully paid tribute to Bon Scott. "Obviously we called the album *Back in Black* because of Bon," said Angus. "We didn't want to just say 'Dedicated to Bon,' because the guy had been with us for five years, and so we all decided it was a far better tribute to him to design the whole album to him rather than just have one little line on the back of the sleeve."

The intensity with which the band worked on the project and the group's sense of having something to prove were made clear in *Back in Black*'s musical contents. The album opened on a chillingly somber note with "Hells Bells," which opens with Angus's slow, mournful guitar weaving around the sounds of bells tolling in tribute to the deceased singer. From the ringing rose the seething tones of the band's new singer. The song, a heartfelt expression of mourning but also a powerful statement of survival and perseverance, rang with familiar force yet was unlike anything the band had previously recorded, and certainly made a strong case for AC/DC's continuing creative vitality.

The entire album was suffused by a double-edged mood of sadness and defiance. Johnson's vocals seethed forcefully on "Shoot to Thrill," "Shake a Leg" and "Let Me Put My Love Into You," while his tart wordplay on "Given the Dog a Bone" and "What Do You Do for Money Honey" maintained AC/DC's tradition of cheeky lyricism. Elsewhere, "Rock and Roll Ain't Noise Pollution" lived up to its title, and the cheerfully lewd "You Shook Me All Night Long" gave AC/DC one of its most infectious tunes yet.

Though it could be interpreted as a fond tribute, the sly "Have a Drink on Me" was taken by some as a distasteful endorsement of the very lifestyle that killed Scott. "A couple of critics thought it was a pretty sick thing to put 'Have a Drink on Me' on the album," Brian acknowledged, adding,

"Everybody was really mad about it, because it's got nothing to do with that at all, absolutely nothing at all. [It's just about] what lads do when they go out for a drink."

Back in Black's monolithic title track—like "Highway to Hell," "Whole Lotta Rosie" and "Riff Raff" before it—had its origins in the band's practice of putting riffs and musical ideas on tape while on the road. "Malcolm [had had the main riff for] 'Back in Black' for about three weeks," Angus told the *Boston Globe.* "He came in one night and said, 'You got your cassette here? Can I put this down? It's been driving me mad. I won't be getting any sleep until I put it on cassette.' He sat down and played it all. The funniest thing is he said to me, 'What do you think? I don't know if it's crap or not, I don't know.' "

Back in Black handily demonstrated just how well Brian Johnson fit into AC/DC—not only as a singer but as a lyricist as well. The new songs demonstrated a singular lyrical sensibility that was distinctive from that of his predecessor, yet equally well suited to the band's collective persona. And if Johnson would never quite equal Scott's exquisitely nasty wit, it's hard to imagine anyone bringing more enthusiasm to the job. "I don't think anybody writing lyrics could miss with those riffs," the singer commented with typical modesty. "You could have written anything and it would have sounded good."

"I think it was professionals meeting up with a rank amateur, myself, and it just meshed," he added. "Just an accident. Just an amateur who thought, 'Well, I'd better write these quick.' The professionals had the gears oiled and it all just fit perfectly."

As Brian explained, "When we started rehearsing, the boys had the riffs and we didn't have any melodies for the songs. They didn't have any tunes. You can write a riff, but you've got to have a tune to go with it, otherwise it's all gonna sound the same. We worked it all out [in rehearsal] and had a basic idea of the tunes we were gonna do before we left for the Bahamas. I had written lyrics for every song, but I knew that the lyrics would have to be vetted by the boys. We just sat around the table and the boys would say, 'I don't like that line, change it,' or they'd come up with an idea."

Though he hadn't been a particularly prolific writer prior to joining AC/DC, Brian shared Bon's humorous attitude toward lyrics. "I've always written songs with tongue in cheek," he said. "Sometimes people ask us what deep message is in the songs, there must be a deep message. No, there's nothing. I just laugh. If you can read something into it, by all means go ahead."

Angus and Malcolm have always insisted they had no interest in "grave-robbing" any of the lyrics that Bon had been working on prior to his death. But according to Scott biographer Clinton Walker, Bon's last girlfriend, Anna Baba, who lived with the singer just prior to his death, claims that his notebooks (which were not among the personal effects delivered to Bon's parents after his death) contained several lyric ideas, including "Rock 'n' Roll Ain't Noise Pollution," that later showed up on *Back in Black.*

The band, meanwhile, claimed that although Bon had left behind a cache of unused lyrics as well as several unissued demo vocals, they decided not to use any of this material, out of respect for their fallen colleague. "A lot of people like to scrape barrels and take whatever they can when someone dies, but we don't want that," said Angus. "It would be like using his death as a means to gain something. If we'd done things in the studio with him, we would possibly have used them, but it's probably best for him too that we won't. There's some stuff

Walking the walk. *(David Corio, Retna)*

of his left, songs off other albums, 'cause we rejected them then and it would just be scraping the barrel. And that's possibly the worst thing that could happen."

Almost immediately upon its release in July 1980—less than six months after Bon shuffled off of this mortal plane—*Back in Black* became an immediate worldwide smash. Over the next decade, it would sell 10 million copies in the U.S. alone. Even American album-rock radio stations sat up and took notice, according the LP a previously unheard-of level of airplay. Meanwhile, "You Shook Me All Night Long" made it to number 20 in the U.K. pop singles charts, followed by "Rock 'n' Roll Ain't Noise Pollution," which climbed to number 15. In short, *Back in Black* firmly established AC/DC as one of the world's biggest rock acts.

As for the band's first tour with its new frontman, Angus predicted, "We'll have to do a lot of the old songs, but we'll have to do a lot of new material too. We're a band famous for the road, and a lot of the old songs are road songs, so it would be like starting all over again if we dropped them. It may be harder that way, but we can only try. It will be difficult at first with the kids seeing someone different onstage, but the thing is we don't want someone who's like Bon as a singer 'cause then we'd get all the comparisons and so on. We'd rather have someone who would sing the songs his way, so we'll probably do a bit more new material to give the guy a chance."

20.

ARE YOU READY?

Any reservations that might have lingered following the musical triumph of *Back in Black* were swiftly quashed after AC/DC played its first live shows with Brian Johnson, breaking in the new lineup with waters-testing concerts in Holland and Belgium before taking on the more intense scrutiny of America and Britain. According to Angus, "Our manager says, 'We don't wanna go anywhere big,' 'cause he didn't know how people were going to react. So it was a small hall, two thousand seats. By the end of the day, the [promoter] says, 'You got fifteen thousand, and they're still coming from all over Europe.' It gave me a good feeling, like maybe we're doing something right."

With Johnson having proven his mettle, the *Back in Black* world tour was undertaken with a vengeance, continuing through the rest of 1980 and into the following year and covering the United States, Britain and Europe, as well as the band's first-ever Japanese dates, and a return—for the first time in over three years—to Australia.

Early in the tour, Johnson reported, "The confidence is building up slowly . . . Every gig I'm doing now is still the first gig, because every audience is a new audience. All the audiences have seen the band before with Bon, so therefore every gig I do is the first time."

The new vocalist was pleasantly surprised by the instant support he received from AC/DC fans. "I remember the first night after we played. I'm not an emotional person by any stretch of the imagination. But the kids had this forty-foot-long banner right across the audience, and it had 'The king is dead; long live the king.' And it was smashing. It was great. And then we went to England and the kids were chanting because they knew how I felt. They knew I was scared.

"Everybody's been dead nice, all of the kids have been great," continued Brian with obvious relief. "I was expecting a few people to maybe say something bad, but nobody has . . . From the first gig—and you've got to remember, the first gigs we did we were doing tracks off *Back in Black* and nobody'd heard them—the reaction was great. It was nice that, as the tour progressed, the album went straight up the charts, and people started to know the songs.

" 'The Jack' was a song we never, ever wanted to do, we thought it was a bit too personal, the way Bon sang it and the personal connotations it had for Bon. But then, about two weeks before we left America, we started to do it and nobody seemed to mind at all, and we did it in England and nobody seemed to mind, and that was it. It was, 'From now on there's nothing that we can't do, because the kids'll accept it.' They're just pleased that AC/DC have kept going. It's been too easy, actually.

"This is the type of band I should have been with years ago," Brian stated. "I can now see that I've been wasting a lot of time during my life. What I really like about the band is that they have no pretensions, they're just four ordinary blokes. When I was with Geordie, you had to teeter around on stack heels and I never liked that."

Brian classified his joining AC/DC as "easy as piss, the easiest band I've ever joined. In other bands, it always took time to get to know people. But in this band, it was always just like going out to the pub and having a drink with a few mates. All that shit about joining a band after somebody else had passed away was just something that anybody would have had to deal with in that situation. I'd be a real wimp if I said, 'Oh, I can't take the pressure; I can't go on . . .'

"The amazing thing about the older stuff," he concluded, "is that when we do a song like 'Let There Be Rock' onstage, sometimes it seems like Bon's ghost is right up there with us. It's a very strange feeling. But we're sure that Bon would have wanted us to keep playing those numbers, and when you see the reaction from the fans, you know that they want us to keep playin' 'em too."

Still, Brian admitted, "If you're alone in the hotel room, and you get up in the morning and look around at your surroundings . . . You come from a working-class family, and you're surrounded by all this kind of thing, and there's limousines outside the door, it's really easy to lose perspective of where you are and what you're doing. But the nice thing about the band is that they're completely down-to-earth, they won't let you escape into that seventh heaven of stardom.

"I remember not so long ago with Geordie we used to play this big club at the top of Gateshead [in Newcastle], and I used to think it was really big-time when we'd get nine hundred people packed in there. Then the next thing I know I'm on the road with these lads, and Philadelphia was one of the first gigs we played. And the first night I walked out in front of all these yelling kids I thought, 'Hey, hang on a minute here, this isn't right.' "

Angus admitted that playing with a new frontman was a big adjustment. "I'd got so used to having Bon there. But Brian's an individual, and that's helped a great deal because he's a pretty natural person. Sometimes Bon would tend to pull back a bit more and then come forward at others. Brian's very much like me—he's got a lot of energy and he's always up front."

Brian, having experienced most of the frustrations that the music business had to offer, was especially appreciative of the devotion of AC/DC's fans. "When they want to find you, they'll let nothing stand in their way," he said. As an example, he pointed to an incident in which a trio of youngsters came knocking on his hotel-room door one night after a show. "There were three fans there who couldn't have been more than twelve years old. I said to 'em, 'Don't you know what time it is?' They said, 'We've been hiding in the broom closet down the hall since this afternoon so we could meet you.' I was pretty mad when they woke me up. After hearing their story all I could do was invite 'em in, order some food from room service and spend some time with 'em. That kind of dedication has to be rewarded."

The *Back in Black* tour also marked the first time that AC/DC had employed onstage visual frills, specifically a huge bronze bell—not a prop, but the genuine article, weighing in at a lean, mean ton and a half—which was lowered at the start of every show and struck repeatedly with a sledgehammer by Johnson in tribute to his departed predecessor. Unfortunately, the bell was too big for the venue when AC/DC played

Brian Johnson's hometown of Newcastle on October 4 and 5.

Additionally, Angus's schoolboy garb had been adapted to include a green velvet uniform and striped tie. And though it would be claimed that it was the Geordie-era Johnson who'd originally inspired Bon to hoist Angus on his shoulders for his nightly venture into the audience, it was now generally left to a roadie to bear that burden.

Joining AC/DC gave Johnson a new appreciation for the talents of his late predecessor. "That poor boy was loved by thousands of people worldwide," he told *Sounds*. "When we did a warm-up gig in Holland, this kid came up to me with a tattoo of Bon on his arm and said, 'This bloke was my hero but now he's gone. I wish you all the luck in the world.' I just stood there shaking; I mean, what can you say when people are prepared to put their faith in you like that? Since then, I feel like I've been singing for that kid and so many others like him. They want the band to go on as well, and certainly I've had no letters or phone calls saying 'Get out.'

"All I can really say is that Bon is still around and watching," he added. "I can't tell you any more because it's all so personal. But at night in my hotel room I had proof that he was there in some form. I know that he approves of what the new lineup is trying to do. He didn't want the band to split up or go into a long period of mourning. He wanted us to build on the spirit he left behind."

In Johnson, AC/DC got a colorful character *minus* the built-in risks that came along with Bon's unpredictable nature. In a 1981 *RAM* interview, he did a good job of expressing the band's attitude toward critics. "With AC/DC it's so easy and simple, critics can't get into it and therefore they can't describe it," he stated. "We just go out and don't give a fuck about critics. We play what we play and that's that."

Indeed, Brian shared Angus and Malcolm's deep distrust of

the media. "I never believed the music press," he claimed. "The only time I buy a music paper is to see who's on where, and the reviews I know are just the personal opinion of one man and not the audience. So therefore, I'm not one who reads reviews. The boys never read reviews. If it's a good one, it's a bonus; you read it and go 'That's nice,' but we generally never go out of our way to read them."

But even the critics had to admit that the band had bounced back in style on the *Back in Black* tour. Reviewing one of the band's three November shows at the London Apollo for England's *Record Mirror,* Fred Williams observed, "Bells toll in black before the band begin, and that's about the only memory of Bon Scott allowed. From here on in it's a trip to the edges of insanity, conducted by vocalist Brian Johnson lurching around like a punch-drunk sailor. Angus Young not so much gripping his guitar as gripped by it, moving around in a fit of demented hysteria in which the only function he's capable of is playing his guitar."

Williams further observed, "It seems that the whole schoolboy element of AC/DC has passed its exams and left school. The bass and rhythm guitarists trot forward in step to sing harmonies, the audience respond to fist-raising gestures with perfect co-ordination . . . Fortunately, the music is strong enough to have survived the showbiz spectacle and present a solid front of aggressive masculinity in which the rhythms are elegant structures from the heart of heavy rock, with the added bonus of more than three chords . . . Anybody doubting the power of music as a socially cohesive force should see an AC/DC show."

AC/DC's retention of its superstar status was demonstrated by the band's impressive showings in year-end press polls. The 1980 year-end *Sounds* heavy-metal poll saw *Back in Black* coming in second in the favorite-album stakes, while Angus finished behind Ritchie Blackmore and Michael Schenker as best guitarist. Meanwhile, the readers of the English hard-rock magazine *Kerrang!* voted *Back in Black* to fourth place in their list of all-time favorite albums.

21

SHAKE YOUR FOUNDATIONS

By 1981 AC/DC had overcome formidable odds to reclaim its place among rock's biggest acts. The band had pulled off one of the most miraculous comebacks in rock history, bouncing back from the death of a key member and coming out of the ordeal more solid—and popular—than ever.

As if any further evidence was needed of AC/DC's preeminence in the early-eighties hard-rock world, one can look to the belated U.S. release of *Dirty Deeds Done Dirt Cheap.* The album, featuring the band's Bon Scott/Mark Evans lineup, zoomed almost instantly to the top of the American charts when Atlantic unleashed it stateside—with its British track sequence, which unfortunately omitted "Jailbreak" while retaining the now-redundant "Problem Child"—in May 1981.

The group had initially resisted Atlantic's interest in exhuming the five-year-old album, fearing that fans would assume that the relatively primitive *Dirty Deeds* was a new album and that the archival material would detract from their efforts to establish their band's current lineup. They eventually consented to the release, provided that the new version bear a reduced list price as well as a sticker reading, "All selections recorded in 1976 by Bon Scott, Angus Young, Malcolm Young, Phil Rudd and Mark Evans."

The music's age aside, *Dirty Deeds'* U.S. release was brilliantly timed, coming at a time when the band's popularity was at its highest. It also didn't hurt that the album's gleefully unsavory title track was one of AC/DC's most memorable anthems; it immediately became one of the band's biggest U.S. airplay hits to date.

One result of the title song's U.S. success was a virtual repeat of the earlier Australian incident in which the "36-24-36" in the lyrics led to telephone troubles. This time, an Illinois couple, Norman and Marilyn White, whose number was close to the aforementioned measurements, filed a $250,000 invasion-of-privacy suit alleging that they had become the target for AC/DC fans with irresponsible dialing fingers. The Whites' suit sought two rather impractical remedies, asking the court to ban the offending song from radio airplay and demanding that the band rerecord the song without the offending number. The latter request would seem particularly difficult, since the song's lead singer had been dead for over a year and a half at the time.

AC/DC's only British appearance of 1981 was on August 8 at the Monsters of Rock festival at Castle Donington in Leicestershire, England, where the band headlined over such notables as Whitesnake, Blue Oyster Cult, Slade and Blackfoot. But AC/DC's triumph was undercut by sound problems, which were exacerbated by the fact that the crowd numbered about eighty thousand rather than the expected fifty thousand, rendering the venue and band's sound equipment insufficient for the occasion.

The Donington festival fell in the midst of the sessions for the next AC/DC album, *For Those About to Rock,* which they and Mutt Lange had begun recording in July in Paris.

Brian Johnson told England's *Record Mirror,* "I was dead pleased with *For Those About to Rock,* because on this album, unlike *Back in Black*—which was composed in such a rush— Angus and Malcolm really took their time. We'd toured constantly for nearly a year and a half, and everybody just wanted a rest. Malcolm and Angus got the riffs together, and I met with them in Paris and we spent about three weeks rehearsing in an old factory outside Paris, and then Mutt came over and we went to the studios.

"But then we suffered a real setback. We just couldn't get the sound together in the studio. It wasn't the live sound we wanted. So we moved to another studio, just as we had to go to Donington. In the end we just reverted to using the old factory that we'd rehearsed in, and it was a great sound there."

The sessions were completed by recording the band in a Paris rehearsal hall, with the help of a mobile studio brought over from England. "We were really pleased with it, you know," Johnson enthused. "Angus and Malcolm wanted to try some real power chords on this album, and I think it came off real brilliant. There are some really classic tracks on there."

Indeed, the album featured the most imposing instrumental tracks the band had yet committed to vinyl, and the songs— featuring some of AC/DC's most rousing choruses yet—were more than a match for the raw, savage sound. The rousing "For Those About to Rock (We Salute You)" opened the album with a rocking call to arms, with Johnson's voice and Angus's and Malcolm's guitars meshing with almost spiritual quality.

Meanwhile, the consistent sonic force and general hook-intensiveness of tunes like "Put the Finger on You," "Let's Get It Up," "Inject the Venom," "Snowballed," "Evil Walks,"

"C.O.D.," "Breaking the Rules," "Night of the Long Knives" and "Spellbound" made it clear that if AC/DC had, as its critics contended, fallen into a formula, it was a *great* formula.

"Put the Finger on You" was, according to Brian Johnson, initially inspired by watching an old James Cagney film on late-night TV. "In one scene, he turns to Bogey and says, 'Watch it buster, or I'm gonna put the finger on you.' Of course, when someone thinks about that song in terms of dealing with a woman, it has a slightly different meaning. Our songs all have a story behind them. They're made to be entertaining, but every time we go into the studio we want to make a song that's a classic."

For Those About to Rock, We Salute You, released November 1981, was an instant smash in the U.S., selling more than a million copies in its first week of release. Within its first month of release, it became the band's first U.S. number 1 album and one of the year's biggest Christmas sellers. *Back in Black* had taken more than a year to go platinum in America; *For Those About to Rock* achieved that distinction less than two months after its release.

AC/DC supported *For Those About to Rock* with its most elaborately staged tour yet, kicking off in the U.S. in the winter of 1981. The show featured full-sized military cannons that were almost—but not quite—as loud as the music, and the usual end-of-show explosions during the encore of the album's title song had to be modified in certain venues due to local fire department regulations. In New Haven, Connecticut, the band was nearly jailed after local fire marshals called in the police, who were waiting when the band stepped offstage. According to Brian, "They had their handcuffs out ready for us and all that shit. They'd already clapped the cuffs on Ian [Jeffery] in fact, and had a gun on his face threatening to stick us all in jail for a year for conspiracy to cause an explosion or something. Crazy!

AC/DC responds to charges that their music objectifies women. (Larry Busacca, Retna)

"That was a strange night for sure," the singer continued. "We had actually finished our set and were just about to come out and play that song when one of our road crew dashed out onstage to tell us that if we fired off the cannons, we'd be arrested. Malcolm, who always loves a good fight, said, 'Let's do it.' But what we didn't know was that the technicians who operate the cannons were being handcuffed backstage just to make sure they didn't try anything. We felt bad about dropping the song from the set that night, but we didn't really have any option. Doing it without the cannons would've been like playing 'Highway to Hell' on acoustic guitars. We'd rather not do anything at all than do it halfway."

Back for a return appearance on the tour was the Hell's Bell, while Angus was now wearing a *red* velvet school uniform. As Dave Lewis noted in *Sounds,* "If anything, Angus seems to be laying on the wild-boy theatrics even thicker these days, writhing epileptically in a heap of thrashing arms and legs on the floor, dashing all over the stage and even up on the speaker stacks at one point, and during 'Bad Boy Boogie' peeling off his tie, jacket and shirt and doing a bump 'n' grind stroll along the front row of clutching hands, twirling his clothes in the air like a bullfighter's cape and catching the arm of his shirt between his legs in a lewd, penis-like gesture. He also cheekily offers to take off his shorts too, sticking his fingers through his fly and finally mooning bare-assed from the drum riser as the band crash back into the riff."

"It's the suit," insisted Angus. "I'm normally the laziest person you'd ever want to meet. But when I put on that school suit, it gets me full of beans. There's something about it. I put it on, and it's probably a bit schizophrenic, but it lets me become someone else for a couple of hours. It never fails to amaze me. When I put it on, I look in the mirror, and I'm afraid."

Despite the increased emphasis on theatrics—not to mention the band's ever-improving chops—AC/DC still played as bluntly and forcefully as ever. Angus: "When you're touring so much, it's hard to prevent yourself getting stale. So I like to think bad. Mean. Think mean, play mean. We like to get the tension up really high and leave it there. Townshend is always violent onstage. He must feel that way to look it and carry it off every time. Sometimes, when I've been playing particularly mean, I have to be guided back to my dressing room because I can't see where I'm going. When I'm onstage, I'll think of anything to keep going. The kids in the audience have come to see you do something wild. They always want to see you better than the last time they saw you."

Despite the tour's masterful melding of visual spectacle and sonic attack, the reviews were often less than appreciative. Writing in the *Washington Post,* critic Richard Harrington dismissed Brian Johnson as sounding "like he gargles with gravel and washes it out with industrial-strength cleaner" and having "Van Gogh's ear for melody and pitch."

Further, Harrington concluded, "AC/DC may be a terrific live band, but their albums are beginning to follow a pathetic formula. Songs like 'Inject the Venom' and 'Breaking the Rules' could serve as parodies of AC/DC . . . What was once exciting heavy metal mayhem is now heavy metal ho-hum."

As usual, Angus was unconcerned with such hairsplitting. "We don't know what people are saying about us. We just like being in the womb of the road. That's the greatest thing for us—going from gig to gig . . . We don't even hear ourselves much on the radio. Every time I turn on the radio, I hear some band like Styx, and I quickly turn it off. That's not rock 'n' roll. That's show business."

In a BBC radio interview in December 1981, Brian Johnson described a surprisingly folksy backstage scene: "You've got the old dart board, in the bar. The great thing is when you go backstage first of all, and you're playin' darts, those five thousand or twenty thousand kids waitin' for you don't seem such a threat anymore. Because you're worryin' about getting through to the next round of the darts final . . . at ten dollars a head, why that's two hundred pounds. It's good because it makes it feel a little bit like home.

"When the lads are on the road in America," Brian admitted, "the pace really does start crippling you, you start not being able to go to sleep until seven in the morning. Your whole life is just totally knocked on the head . . . You snap out of it when the curtains open; you hear the crowd startin' to go crazy, you realize this is for real. And you've got to get down to some hard work."

"We are a club band, even though we don't play clubs anymore," Malcolm stated. "I know a lot of big bands who would never survive playing a club gig. I think people watch us and say to themselves, 'Oh, look at those poor buggers, they think they're playing in a club,' when we might be playing to ten thousand or twenty thousand people. You can't help but sympathize with an act like that—it's as simple as that.

"As long as you stick to your original plan of what to do, which is simply just to play, then that's the whole bottom of it," insisted Malcolm. "Just to get up onstage and put on a good show, it doesn't matter what's being said or not said about you."

"To the kids in the audience, AC/DC pose no threat," said Brian. "I mean, they can look up and say, 'That could be me. I could be that guitarist . . . And that singer, he doesn't look any smarter than me—in fact, I look smarter than him. That rhythm guitarist, all he's got on is a pair of jeans, T-shirt and pumps,' and that's what they're standing there for."

22

NERVOUS SHAKEDOWN

The spring of 1982 saw the belated—and rather brief—U.S. theatrical release of *AC/DC: Let There Be Rock,* the low-budget concert film comprised of footage shot in France in 1979, shortly before Bon Scott's death. For the occasion, theaters were specially outfitted with banks of 2,500- to 5,000-watt five-way speakers—dubbed the Wall of Sound—that attempted to replicate the AC/DC live experience as the band performed "Live Wire," "Shot Down in Flames," "Let There Be Rock," "Hell Ain't a Bad Place to Be," "Sin City," "Walk All Over You," "Blink of an Eye," "The Jack," "High Voltage," "Whole Lotta Rosie," and "Rocker"—featuring a brief shot of Angus running to catch a whiff from the oxygen tank he kept nearby for occasions when his adrenaline got the better of him.

The critics were not impressed. The *New York Times'* Stephen Holden called *Let There Be Rock* "a dull, cheaply made concert film that should appeal only to diehard fans."

Holden further noted, "Technically, the movie is not all it's cracked up to be. The so-called Wall of Sound . . . is loud, but it doesn't come close to capturing the reverberating thunder that can make arena rock so viscerally exciting. And in many of the concert scenes the soundtrack is noticeably out of synch with what's on the screen.

"Ideally," Holden observed, "a filmed rock concert should try to bring out the interrelationship among the musicians and to suggest how the music works, both on a technical and emotional level. *AC/DC: Let There Be Rock,* however, doesn't even begin such an exploration."

Aside from *Let There Be Rock*'s brief theatrical run, AC/DC stayed out of the public eye for most of 1982, during which time they wrote, rehearsed and recorded new material, this time without the help of an outside producer. The band reemerged in August 1983 with a new album, *Flick of the Switch,* whose production was credited to the entire band.

"A lot of people thought Mutt Lange *made* AC/DC, and that was a real pain," groaned Angus. "Mutt had never really worked with a rock 'n' roll band before us . . . I'm not takin' anything away from him, and I'll give him credit for what he does. He knows what he wants soundwise and he knows what he wants vocally. But he never really had a chance to be the boss with us, because we weren't inclined in his way. If we had worked the way Mutt wanted, it would have been a lot more glossy and sheened up.

"When we worked with our brother, he used to let us do a lot of our own stuff. But when we were working with Mutt, we had to do a lot of battling for what we wanted. *Back in Black* was our biggest album [in the U.S.], and Malcolm took care of a lot of the songs on that album because Mutt didn't really understand them. We always knew what we wanted, and it always came down to what we put into it. And the further we got on, the more we ended up doing things by ourselves. It's a funny thing—you work with some of these guys for years, listening to them telling you to do this and that, and then you realize that you could always see what was needed."

Like its simple pencil-drawing cover, *Flick of the Switch* stripped AC/DC back down to its basic elements while retaining the key lessons learned from the band's work with Lange. "We wanted it to sound a bit rawer and we wanted a very tough album," said Angus. "We've always had that sound and we've always been very hard with it, but this time we wanted to make it really tough. I think the kids see it too, when they hear it and everything. They've got a feeling that it was done by these guys because they wanted it to be done this way."

True to Angus's word, *Flick of the Switch* was one of AC/DC's most energetic efforts yet, with songs like "Rising Power," "This House Is on Fire," "Flick of the Switch," "Nervous Shakedown," "Guns for Hire" and "Brain Shake" showcasing a trimmer, scaled-down sound that was perfectly suited to live performance.

"Most people, when they progress, they progress up their own asses," Malcolm said by way of explanation.

"Critics can put the records down," said Angus. "They're not buying them. It's the people who buy 'em. They can criticize all they want."

But people *weren't* buying *Flick of the Switch,* at least not in the numbers to which the band had grown accustomed. If *For Those About to Rock* was unquestionably a smash, it was also the first AC/DC album not to outsell the AC/DC album before it. The downward sales trend continued with *Flick of the Switch.* Though the collection managed to make it into the U.S. Top 10, its commercial performance was noticeably lackluster in comparison to its blockbuster predecessors.

Flick of the Switch also marked the final recorded appearance of Phil Rudd, whose pneumatic thump had long been the rock-solid foundation upon which AC/DC's guitar and vocal mayhem was built. Following the album's completion, Rudd—the band's last remaining Australian member—either quit or was given the boot, depending on whom you believe. "He was thinking about [leaving] for a while," Angus said. "He didn't mind the studio side of it; it was the touring that did it. He likes toying with his yachts better."

Into the breach stepped twenty-year-old Englishman Simon Wright (born while Bon Scott was doing time in Riverbank), who was recruited through a musician-wanted ad in time to tour behind the new album. "We just put an ad in the paper saying, 'Any drummer under five feet two inches,'" claimed Angus.

According to Wright, "I saw an ad in a British music paper that said, 'Rock group looking for a drummer.' I never dreamed it would be AC/DC. I made a phone call and then I went to a rehearsal—there were Brian, Angus, Malcolm and Cliff. I couldn't believe my eyes. We went through a first rehearsal, and things went very well. They invited me back, and the second time I was very nervous. But they obviously liked what I played, so I got the job."

Despite *Flick of the Switch*'s disappointing sales, fans still turned out in reasonably healthy numbers for the accompanying tour, which featured return appearances by the by-now-familiar bell and cannons. One visitor on the U.S. tour was Brian Johnson's dad. "I was at Monte Cassino when the Americans flattened the place, and I was at El Alamein when we knocked Rommel back with a big barrage of guns," the elder Johnson told *People* magazine. "But I've never heard anything as loud as this in my life."

As usual, though, the stage frills were always overshadowed by Angus Young (whose stage presence *People* had described as "Tweedledum on acid"), whose hyperkinetic movements and motley striptease remained AC/DC's most spectacular special effects. "I don't know why I do it," he said of his strip act. "I just do not know. I think it might be 'cause of the drums, you know. It's always when I hear those drums pounding away. I mean, I've walked onstage and said to everyone, 'I am not going to do it,' and bam, I end up doing it . . . Whether I do it depends on how up the audience is, and I used to have more fun doing it to people who never knew what was going to happen. The good thing is that it does take away a lot of the serious side to the show 'cause people can have a laugh at it. I mean, I can't imagine Mick Jagger or someone like that doing it."

Angus's Dutch-born wife, Ellen, has admitted to fearing for her husband's safety when watching him perform. "I get scared every time he falls to the floor," she said. "It's not just a stunt. He really falls out there." Indeed, Angus's knees by now were callused from repeatedly hitting the ground, and he'd chipped several teeth hitting himself with his guitar.

The guitarist's demented-schoolboy image has become so all-encompassing that the diminutive axeman is rarely recognized when he's offstage and out of uniform. Apparently, his bigger-than-life persona makes people expect him to be taller. "Some of the women that used to come looking for me [after concerts] were like Amazons," he once commented. "I'd open the door and say, 'It's okay, I'm just his butler.' "

The guitarist's manic performing style is all the more impressive in that it is achieved without the aid of any substance stronger than tea. By rock 'n' roll standards, at least, Angus is something of a health freak. "I was brought up in a different lifestyle," he says. "I like fresh food, fresh bread and fresh milk. In [America], we always seem to get stuck with fast food. Even the milk is wrong; it seems to have vitamin D or something else added. It tastes watery."

As for the nonchemical forms of on-the-road carousing available to red-blooded male rock stars, Brian Johnson has stated, "I never touch 'em. I'm a married man with two kids. Anyway, there are just too many nasty diseases goin' around America to take any chances. I'll offer 'em a hearty handclasp and that's about it. We're all good boys in this band. We only like good, clean fun, like a game of cards."

Former producer Mutt Lange confirmed this somewhat disturbing image of the members of AC/DC as nice, clean-living young men. "You have this image of them as hell-raisers, but they all stand up for a lady. In fact, they were much too polite."

Or, as one record company spokesman put it, "AC/DC is the kind of band that would think twice before bending the corner on a room-service menu."

"You can only be yourself, and not worry about what's being created image-wise or whatever," Angus stated. "You always get the people who say, 'Oh, there's a rock 'n' roll band, look out, any moment now a TV set is going to go out the window!' And Malcolm said, 'What for? That's a waste of a good TV!' Everyone sort of looks for that angle, for a scandal, for the sex, the drugs and the rock 'n' roll. I think with AC/DC, it's the rock 'n' roll. I don't mind the first one every now and again. But the drugs I can do without, thank you."

Aside from his prodigious intake of tea, Angus's only known vice is cigarettes, a habit he describes as something of a family tradition. "I think everyone in my family smokes, except my mother," he told *Musician*. "My father was the only man I ever saw who could smoke in his sleep. He died of lung cancer. He was a spray painter in a factory. In those days, they didn't have masks, so eventually the doctors told him he'd have to stop for the health of his lungs. I wouldn't want for anyone to start smoking, but when I started, it was encouraged. I could buy cigarettes from the age of fourteen and nobody questioned it."

Incidentally, Angus traces his oft voiced disdain for drugs back to the sixties. "When I was growing up," he explained to *Spin,* "all those hippie bands were popular. They'd always be playing stoned—I thought they were fuckin' horrible. They sounded like shit, and I hated it. I always thought drugs were a waste of time."

That feeling was strengthened by the losses that AC/DC suffered due to substance abuse. "Bon died because of alcohol, and that whole period had a big effect on my life," he says. "It was a real tragedy; he was really close to me. I really came to realize how fragile life can be, and how quickly you can lose it all. Personally, I was never really involved in drugs and drinking. I have enough trouble getting up in the morning without any of that. I've seen so many people over the years fade away because of their bad habits. It's really not worth it—there's so many other things to worry about when you're trying to do this for a living that you can't be bothered with that crap."

23
GUNS FOR HIRE

In the absence of a new album for 1984, AC/DC returned to the European festival circuit, including a performance at the annual Monsters of Rock festival at England's Castle Donington, where they headlined over the likes of Motley Crüe, Ozzy Osbourne and Van Halen. By this time, the band had an album's worth of new songs written, but, true to their policy of not playing unfamiliar material in concert, none of the new songs were unveiled.

"We've never believed in playing songs in concert that nobody knows," stated Brian. "The fans come to hear the ones they know, the old things. We'd be taking advantage if we played new things to them. We are looking forward to finishing work on the new material and then playing those songs on our next tour. We'll be in America by spring, and that's when everyone will hear the new songs played live. And I can tell you that they won't be disappointed."

In the meantime, American fans were blessed with the release of *'74 Jailbreak,* an EP collecting five vintage Bon Scott–era tracks previously unavailable in the U.S. Alongside the landmark "Jailbreak"—featured on the Australian edition of *Dirty Deeds Done Dirt Cheap* but inexplicably deleted from the U.S. version—were "You Ain't Got a Hold on Me," "Show Business," "Soul Stripper" and "Baby, Please Don't Go," all drawn from the Australian *High Voltage.*

As if the band's declining record sales weren't a big enough cause for concern, the eighties saw the rise of another distressing AC/DC-related activity. Now that they'd finally begun to earn the respect of the rock critics who'd originally condemned them for simplemindedness or sexism, they would have to contend with a new, wholly more intolerant group of critics who would claim that AC/DC was not merely lacking in imagination or finesse but in league with Satan himself.

Since the early days of rock 'n' roll, blaming the music for society's ills has been a popular pursuit in the United States. In the eighties a combination of conservative extremists and religious zealots launched another wave of antirock (and implicitly procensorship) hysteria. A United Press International story dated November 1, 1981, for instance, reported on the efforts of a Dallas minister, James "Gibby" Gilbert, to expose the evils of subliminal and "backwards masked" messages supposedly contained within popular rock albums.

Though Gilbert did not single out any instances of either subliminal or backwards messages on AC/DC discs, he did helpfully point out that the group's name "denotes bisexuality, and the dash between AC and DC is a satanic 'S.'" The minister further claimed that "groups like Led Zeppelin, Fleetwood Mac, the Eagles and the Rolling Stones . . . are really into the occult."

AC/DC was regularly singled out for its supposed use of sexual and "satanic" imagery. At one point someone decided that the band's name was short for "Anti-Christ/Devil's Children" or "Anti-Christ/Devil's Crusade," while others interpreted songs like "Highway to Hell," "Hells Bells," "Hell Ain't a Bad Place to Be," "Rock 'n' Roll Damnation" and "C.O.D." (Care of the Devil) as oaths of loyalty to the dark overlord himself.

But, as AC/DC fans are well aware, "Highway to Hell" was not intended as an invocation of dark forces, but rather an evocation of the more mundane "hell" of the early AC/DC's endless low-budget tours. "It has nothing to do with devil worship," an exasperated Angus told the *Los Angeles Times.* "We toured for four years at a stretch with no break. A guy asked how would you best describe our tours. We said, 'A highway to hell.' The phrase stuck with us."

"All we'd done," moaned Angus, "is describe what it's like to be on the road for four years. When you're sleeping with the singer's socks two inches from your nose, believe me, that's pretty close to hell."

As for "Hell Ain't a Bad Place to Be," Angus said, "That song is a joke. We're saying if you've got the choice between heaven and hell, you might pick hell. In heaven you have harp music and in hell there's a good rocking band and rocking songs. That's what we'd choose. So hell ain't a bad place to be. It's all in fun."

The band was typically blunt in its response to its accusers, dismissing them as crackpots with questionable motives. "Those God-botherers mention the devil more than we do," said Brian. "They're just trying to scare people. The big idea with us isn't satanic messages. It's trying to get one line to rhyme with the next."

"We're not black magic satanists," Angus echoed. "I don't drink blood. I may wear black underpants now and again, but that's it."

Though AC/DC has generally been careful to maintain an apolitical stance, the band's interviews on this subject are probably the closest they've ever come to taking a public stand on a topical issue. Speaking to American journalist Harold De-Muir, Brian Johnson was clear in his contempt for the evangelists, with "their personalized designer churches," who encouraged such activity. "They're screwin' people into sending them money. *That's* pornography.

"I turned on the TV and there was one of them at Madison Square Garden," Brian recounted, "and he was using all these old clichés that bands used to use. He says, 'I don't care what they say about New York, this is the friendliest city I've ever been to,' and the audience went apeshit. And I saw this other guy who openly said, 'I saw God last night—he came to me in a dream, and he talked to me.' That's blasphemy! If God was gonna come down and talk to somebody, the last person he'd talk to is a guy with a fleet of Cadillacs, who claims to have had a runnin' conversation with him for the last fifteen years."

Nonetheless, antirock propagandists targeted AC/DC sporadically through the 1980s, sometimes picketing the band's U.S. shows. "Most of the kids just laughed at them," reported Brian, "but it could have been a very dangerous situation. Those people were trying to show that our music was going to corrupt the soul of everyone who listened to it. But I don't think that anyone who comes to our show is about to let a piece of paper convince them not to come.

"Those fanatical groups followed us from city to city handing out their material," continued the singer. "Thankfully, they didn't get hurt. The only place I heard there was any trouble was in Cleveland, where some of our fans took exception to what they were doing and tried in a rather physical way to convince them to stop. I'm a man of peace, but in my heart I wish I could have been out there with 'em that night."

In an interview with *Musician* magazine, Angus demonstrated the distrust of organized religion that he and Malcolm had had instilled in them since childhood, stating that he didn't believe particularly in God or Satan. "I believe in common sense. I think people just need to think there's an afterlife, 'cause it would throw them if everything just went black at the end. My father wouldn't let us go to church when we were little. You've got that Catholic/Protestant thing in Northern Ireland, and it spilled over into Glasgow. There used to be a lot of gang fights, and he thought it was all bullshit."

By the mid-1980s the members of AC/DC had more enjoyable extramusical interests than Satan worship. Angus had taken up a new and quite unmenacing hobby of painting landscapes that he described as "happy atmospheric street scenes," adding, "I like to paint landscape things, like mountains, flowers and trees—nothing too elaborate." He has, however, been known to draw a trademark mischievous cartoon devil in a schoolboy uniform. Brian, meanwhile, spent his off-hours working on motorcycles and studying military history.

24

DEEP IN THE HOLE

AC/DC launched 1985 with a bang, performing before a record crowd of 400,000 fans at the Rock in Rio festival, on a bill that also included the Scorpions, Ozzy Osbourne and Whitesnake. Following the festival, the band packed up for Mountain Studios in Montreux, Switzerland, to start work on their next album, once again with Angus and Malcolm handling production duties.

The album, *Fly on the Wall,* arrived in June 1985, sporting worthy new riff-monsters like "Shake Your Foundations," "Sink the Pink," "Danger," "First Blood" and "Playing With Girls." *Creem*'s Jim Farber described the album, with some accuracy, as sounding "like a horde of rabid dogs racing through a hall of razor blades, only catchier."

Though it would prove to be one of AC/DC's weaker sellers, *Fly on the Wall* nonetheless possessed considerable musical merit, maintaining the band's low-tech, high-energy integrity. "It's a natural thing with us," said Angus. "Even in the early days, we never bothered with any effects or distortion boosters or crap on that end. . . . That's the sort of band we always were. We don't go, 'Let's use the latest sound.' "

Once again, Angus gave copious credit to brother Malcolm (aka "the Riffmaker") for the fat, infectious guitar lines that have always been the foundation of AC/DC's sound. "I can churn out hundreds of riffs," Angus said, "but he'll come up with one and once you hear it, you'll go 'shit.' He has that classic guitar feel—like in a song like 'Back in Black' or 'Fly on the Wall.' . . . A lot of people don't appreciate what rhythm guitar is."

According to a June 1985 survey by the music-industry trade magazine *Billboard,* AC/DC was the world's best-selling hard-rock act, boasting worldwide sales of 25 to 30 million albums, placing them ahead of the likes of Van Halen, Def Leppard, Rush and Led Zeppelin. But the strength of AC/DC's catalogue wasn't reflected in the declining sales of their new releases. Though *Flick of the Switch*'s sales had been worrisome, falling short of the million mark, *Fly on the Wall*'s were—at least by AC/DC standards—downright disastrous, selling just over half a million.

Angus, at least publicly, was philosophical about the dip in sales. "Everybody goes up and down," he said. "We just try to play our music and not worry about anything else.

"*Back in Black* is our most successful album in the States, so many of our fans base [their expectations] on that. But we were around long before *Back in Black.* In America people tend to associate wealth with success, whereas in other parts of the world success has more to do with making something that satisfies you."

Brian Johnson, as much a product of the working class as the Young brothers, expressed a similar skepticism toward success. "After you've been in the first [limo], it's just a thing, you know. Because it's not yours, it doesn't belong to you, and you know that in two months time you could be back in your little old Ford Popular. [Success] is such a fickle thing, and the good thing about AC/DC is that they treat it as such."

It was with *Fly on the Wall* that AC/DC finally dove whole hog into the world of conceptual music video, which they'd largely resisted up until that point, with the notable exception of the 1976 "Jailbreak" clip. "It's great for corn flakes!" Angus said of the much-maligned medium. "For some things it's great to see a visual, as long as you can make it like a record. A lot of people don't care. Some people use it as art and just go along with the directors to make money. I feel sorry for some of those people."

Despite Angus and Malcolm's oft-stated disdain for the rock-video form, the band made good use of it with a long-form video produced in conjunction with *Fly on the Wall.* The five-song presentation, shot in World's End, a seedy club on Manhattan's Lower East Side, featured a drunken cartoon fly veering through the lives of various dodgy characters while AC/DC did its stuff on stage.

Unfortunately, a considerably graver issue loomed on the horizon. On August 31, 1985, Los Angeles police apprehended Richard Ramirez, the "Night Stalker" who had murdered at least a dozen people during a reign of terror that had begun eight months earlier. The sign of the pentagram—the five-pointed star associated with witchcraft and Satan worship—had been found painted at some of the crime scenes. Police had also found an AC/DC cap at the site of one of the murders.

It turned out that Ramirez had been obsessed with the supposed "satanic" imagery featured on the *Highway to Hell* album, and particularly with the lyrics of "Night Prowler," which had actually been written about a Peeping Tom. The band's tangential involvement in the Ramirez case won AC/DC a new level of unwanted celebrity, giving pause to some of those who'd earlier dismissed the claims of satanic imagery and backwards masking as ridiculous.

The band, under fire in the wake of the Night Stalker case, initially met questions about the case with a terse "no comment," but eventually Angus went public to rebut the charges that he and his band were leading America's youth down the path to degeneracy and murder. "I'd heard that about this killer running around California and doing people," said Angus. "I should have realized, put two and two together, when they started talking about satanic cults. I knew they'd come after us."

But nothing Angus could say could stop certain sectors of the public from mentally associating AC/DC with the actions of a serial killer, as the band found out when they toured America in support of *Fly on the Wall.* The City Council of Springfield, Illinois—the hometown of Abe Lincoln—failed in its attempt to ban the group's concert there, but the band members were informed that they would be held individually liable if the show had to be stopped. The band later complained that the concert's less-than-capacity turnout (about five thousand fans in an eight-thousand-seat venue) was due to confusion over whether the show was on or off.

As for the Springfield City Council, Angus commented, "They're the ones who were breaking the law. We're protected by the First Amendment, which supports freedom of speech. After the council banned the show, we had to spend a week with all the legal hassles of getting the show back on. These people are so high-and-mighty. . . . They should be cleaning up their town instead of picking on us."

Later on in California, some Orange County residents managed to get AC/DC's October 21 Pacific Amphitheater show canceled due to the band's vague connections to the Night Stalker case.

With *People* magazine doing a cover story asking "Has rock gone too far?" and reporting rumors that the families of Ramirez's victims were considering suing the band, rock critics—of all people—found themselves springing to AC/DC's defense en masse. "The message is rebellion, not devil worship," pointed out *Los Angeles Times* critic Robert Hilburn.

"Heavy metal may be the music that can't get no respect," wrote the *Washington Post*'s Richard Harrington, "but in the past six years, it's had no trouble getting attention." Harrington further observed, "Someone once said heavy metal was invented to reassure adolescent boys who have limited experience with women that they're not gay, and there certainly is a blatant misogyny at the root of the music—which may explain why AC/DC fans are overwhelmingly young males. But AC/DC's real force comes from the power chords, shout-along choruses and a deafening, incapacitating decibel level that millions of adolescents seem to thrive on."

"It gives them energy," agreed Angus. "They can swing their arms, bang their chairs, jump around. It's a form of getting rid of steam. Then they go home happy."

Angus assured the *Los Angeles Times* that the band was not about to tone down its music to placate its detractors. "We're not going to put out something totally bland just to avoid being hassled. But I have a feeling now it doesn't matter what we do. If we sang about flowers and trees, people would find something in the song to connect us to Satan."

Angus seemed accustomed to being judged by the pillars of "straight" society. "If I sit down on an airplane, I know the guy sitting next to me is thinking, 'He's gotta be a hippie dropout

Showbiz professional that he is, Angus refuses to let the fact that
a ton-and-a-half bronze bell is hanging directly above his noggin
affect his performance. *(Larry Busacca, Retna)*

dope pusher.' They love me when I walk through customs at airports—'Come with me, sir.'

"It's always the one they think's not who's the one that is," Angus continued. "We used to get taught in school not to judge a book by its cover, but that's exactly what these same people do when they see us. A lot of people think you're dumb— you're in a rock 'n' roll band, so you're nothing more than five dumb guys that some record company's stuck together. We've never done much schooling, but that never stopped me from readin' books, and we're not stupid.

"Brian and Malcolm both have kids, and their kids look up to them and respect them. I think they stand out a lot more than these ordinary people ever will, because they've done something, and all these people have ever done is follow the rest of the sheep."

Still, it was undeniable that the members of AC/DC were coming dangerously close to being respectable members of society. All but drummer Wright were married, and Malcolm and Brian were fathers of two children each.

Brian Johnson, now residing in Fort Myers, Florida, admitted, "It's very cold and damp in the north of England, and I was sick of saying how wonderful it was up there."

25
SHAKE A LEG

By 1987 mainstream hard rock often sounded like a pale shadow of its former self, with the genre increasingly dominated by carefully manicured combos who emphasized slickly produced radio fodder over honestly sweaty rock 'n' roll. But, despite the substandard sales of *Flick of the Switch* and *Fly on the Wall,* AC/DC steadfastly refused to soften its approach in an attempt to broaden its commercial appeal.

"It wouldn't be AC/DC if we did something completely different," said Angus. "And we're certainly not going to start putting dragons on the album covers."

In laying out the band's musical philosophy, Angus stated that AC/DC songs "have to swing. When we write songs, the first thing is the feel. It's got to have that bottom edge to it and you take it from there . . . It's dumb to make a song fast just for the sake of being fast . . . The bottom line is we get out there and play rock 'n' roll music. I may wear that school suit, but for me that just gives me that extra confidence. Then I can act like a real asshole."

In interviews, Angus, as always, would seem hard-pressed to name any current bands or artists that he actually liked, still naming Chuck Berry as his idol. "I've always liked his music because it's simple and direct," he told *Request.* "You don't have to think about it. It makes you dance and tap your feet. I've never been impressed with someone who can zoom up and down [the guitar neck]. I can do that myself, but I call it practicing."

"I've always maintained that rock can be tough and hard without being doom and gloom metal," Angus told the *Toronto Star.* "To me, a lot of that heavy stuff leaves me feeling like I've seen a bad B-movie. But that's always been the case. When we started, everyone I knew was raving about Jimi Hendrix, and I was going around telling them, 'Hey, now Chuck Berry can write a song.' "

When it came to drawing the line between hard rock and heavy metal, Angus made it clear that AC/DC considers itself to be the former. "We believe, first and foremost, that it's gotta have that swing. I always looked at the metal thing more as music by numbers. It's devoid, actually, of a lot of feeling. It's more concentrating on technique—like now you see a lot of them going at it fast and furious."

"It's hard rock," agreed Brian. "It's nothing like heavy metal, 'cause heavy metal bores me to tears, it really does. I just cannot listen to it. I can't enjoy it. There is a distinguishing point between the two, definitely, and I think the kids know that. You can tell it a mile off. When I start wearing tight silk trousers and studs on me arms and studded belts and things like that, then I'll turn heavy metal."

But even the stubborn Young brothers must have realized that it might not be a bad thing to reassess some of their preconceptions regarding AC/DC's longstanding insularity. So when superstar horror author (and AC/DC fan) Stephen King invited the band to contribute some new music to his debut as a film director, *Maximum Overdrive,* they agreed.

As if the occasion of AC/DC's first movie sound track assignment wasn't historic enough, the *Maximum Overdrive* project also saw the band reunite with the production team of Harry Vanda and George Young for the first time in eight years. They recorded three new tracks with Vanda and Young: "Who Made Who"—their most infectious tune in ages—along with the slow-burning "D.T." and the muscular guitar instrumental "Chase the Ace."

Although *Maximum Overdrive* bombed at the box office, the project was a boon for the band, with "Who Made Who" emerging as its biggest hit in years, with a video featuring a multitude of head-banging Angus clones. The film spawned an all-AC/DC sound track album, *Who Made Who,* released in May 1986, combining the three new songs with the vintage "You Shook Me All Night Long," "Hells Bells" and "For Those About to Rock," the recent "Sink the Pink" and "Shake Your Foundations" and the positively ancient Bon Scott–era chestnut "Ride On."

Flush from the platinum success of *Who Made Who,* the band brought Vanda and Young back for the next full-length AC/DC effort, *Blow Up Your Video,* released in January 1988. The album, complete with a flamboyant cover shot of Angus bursting through a giant TV screen, featured a spacious, live-sounding ambience, inventive riffage and old-fashioned raw enthusiasm that animated tracks like "That's the Way I Wanna Rock 'n' Roll," "Meanstreak," "Kissin' Dynamite" and the hit "Heatseeker."

Apparently, Harry and George weren't the only old associates to return to the fold for the *Blow Up Your Video* sessions.

Angus suggested that the band had been visited in the studio by the spirit of the departed Bon Scott. "You hear eerie things, spiritual things," he told *Musician*'s Charles M. Young. "Sometimes you're sitting in a recording studio, and you can hear another voice singing in the backing track . . . I don't know, it might all be in my head. Sometimes you hear things—it might even be on the radio—and you just do a double take. But is there an afterlife? I don't know. Nobody's ever come back to tell what it's like. Maybe we all become insects."

When AC/DC hit the road again in the spring of 1988, it was without Malcolm Young, who reportedly sat out the tour in order to attend to his ill son. The band's choice of replacement kept things in the family—Angus and Malcolm's nephew Stevie Young, who did his best to approximate the Riffmaker's trademark sound by borrowing Malcolm's vintage Gretsch guitars and Marshall amps.

Malcolm's absence made it clear to Angus just how essential his older brother, whom he's called "the best rhythm player in the business," is to AC/DC's overall sound. "Malcolm has never gotten the credit he deserves," Angus later told *Hit Parader.* "He's an incredible songwriter, and an amazing rhythm guitarist. Playing that kind of guitar takes a special person, and Malcolm has just the right feel for it. He's been willing to live a little bit in my shadow over the years, but [touring] without him just reinforced what I already knew—he's a very important member of the band.

"Malcolm," Angus said, "is a big inspiration to me. He can always tell me if I'm playing good or bad. He's a very tough critic. I know if I can please Malcolm I can please the world. A lot of people say, 'AC/DC—that's the band with the little guy who runs around in shorts.' But I wouldn't be able to do it without Malcolm and the other guys pumping out the rhythm. They make me look good."

In another interview, Brian Johnson insisted that, unlike most rock frontmen, he's perfectly comfortable taking a backseat to his band's lead guitarist. "We're different from any other band," he said. "There's no frontman out there all the time hogging the spotlight and swearing. Everybody else does it, though. I think there's a school for it. One of our guys used to work for this band—I won't mention their name—and the singer said 'fuck' 165 times during one show. That was the record. Our guy used to count 'fucks' every night with a clicker.

"I've never said 'fuck' onstage," he added. "Well, I said it once. And this woman said, 'I can't believe you swore onstage. I've my daughter here.' And I said, 'Jeez, I'm sorry,' and I've never said it since. In fact, I never say anything onstage. The music's supposed to do the talking."

In March 1988 London's *Financial Times* reviewed the Malcolmless AC/DC show at Wembley Arena and noted that AC/DC "has been mounting the same show for over a decade now" but that Angus "has progressed a bit. He used to perform in flannel shorts, school blazer and cap. Now he wears a green velveteen suit, though still cuts it off well above the knee. He also matches the audience in outrage, stripping off for a quick 'moon,' while indulging in other unnatural practices like strutting across stage like a street walker and dashing around like a headless chicken."

In January 1989 AC/DC achieved one of the odder distinctions of its career when U.S. troops used "Highway to Hell" at top volume to coax deposed Panamanian dictator Manuel Noriega out of his refuge at Panama's Vatican Embassy—conclusively proving that AC/DC still had the ability to annoy the right people. "They were trying to aggravate him so he couldn't get a restful sleep," Angus explained. "It was pretty funny for us. I figure if our music is good enough for the U.S. Army, it's good enough for anybody, I guess."

"When I heard that," added Brian, "my first thought was, now we'll never get to play for the pope."

Otherwise, the band took most of 1989 off, while various rumors of internal troubles made the rounds. Malcolm eventually returned to the fold. Brian, who'd moved to Florida to escape Britain's high tax rates, got divorced. And Simon Wright left to join Dio.

With some breathing space built into their schedule for a change, the Young brothers concentrated on writing new songs without the usual deadline pressures. "We had plenty of time, which was good," Angus said. "In the past, we've always been committed to something; sometimes we've even been committed to touring, with the dates set, and we wouldn't even be finished with the record. This time, there was no pressure on us, which was great. We could write songs, take some time and listen to them, say 'That's good' or 'That needs help,' maybe change a piece here or there. We don't really like to go into the studio with nothing and try to do it there. We like to have it done and worked out, so that when you're recording, you can concentrate on the performance and the sound."

26
SHOOT TO THRILL

In 1990 a feature in *Request* magazine caught the members of AC/DC in the out-of-character act of schmoozing with British record retailers at a fancy restaurant, to promote their new album, titled—with the band's usual disregard for punctuation—*The Razors Edge*. At some point in the proceedings, a sullen Malcolm Young chided the more outgoing Brian Johnson for looking like he was having a good time. "You don't *like* this shit, do you?" the guitarist asked the singer.

It wouldn't be long before AC/DC—now managed by Los Angeles–based Englishman Stewart Young (no relation)—would once again be in a position to refuse to submit to such promotional activity, thanks to their September 1990 release *The Razors Edge*. The album was originally slated to have been produced by the Vanda/Young team, but early on in the project, the pair were sacked once again and replaced by Canadian hard-rock specialist Bruce Fairbairn.

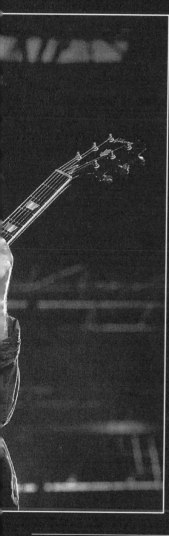

Angus and pal. *(Pentti Hokkanen, S.I.N.)*

The album also saw the arrival of new drummer Chris Slade, a chrome-domed English vet whose résumé includes membership in Manfred Mann's Earth Band and the ill-starred Jimmy Page/Paul Rodgers "supergroup" the Firm. "His style is just perfect for the band; it's as solid and powerful as you can get," Angus said of Slade. "Chris is a bit similar to Phil Rudd; they both smash the drums as hard as they can. But Chris can be frightening to look at—you look at his bald head and it could scare you."

Producer Fairbairn, though best known for adding a digitally slick, radio-friendly sheen to such bands as Aerosmith, Bon Jovi and Poison, managed to retain AC/DC's raw edge while emphasizing the sharp hooks of such tunes as "Thunderstruck," "Moneytalks," "Fire Your Guns," "Are You Ready" and the seasonal specialty "Mistress for Christmas," which added sleighbells to the AC/DC lineup.

"His name got called out a lot, so Malcolm went to Vancouver to meet with him," Angus said of Fairbairn. "Bruce told Malcolm that he didn't want to change AC/DC, and he didn't want us to do anything that we'd be uncomfortable with. These days it's hard to find people who are rock producers. A lot of people say they are, but as soon as you start working with them they'll push their ballads at you.

"The material was all ready to go when we got to Vancouver," continued Angus. "[Fairbairn] just brought out the dynamics a bit. Bruce is a big fan of our older albums; he said he liked the excitement, rawness and lack of production on them. He wanted to capture that in-your-face sound again and did a good job doing it. There were very few overdubs. But sometimes somebody had picked their nose and hit the wrong chord, so we patched up a couple of songs."

According to Brian, "The studio experience reminded me of the old days when we would experiment with the arrangements and just try things out for the fun of it. In the back of our minds, we realized that there is a whole generation of fans that has sprung up in the three years since our last album was released. I want them to see what all this noise and fun is all about."

For the first time in AC/DC's history, Angus and Malcolm wrote all of the album's lyrics—a job that had originally been the responsibility of Bon Scott and that was subsequently inherited by Brian Johnson. But this time around, the distractions of a painful divorce battle kept Brian from performing his duties as lyricist, and the Young brothers took up the slack. "I just said, 'Gee, guys, this is great. I'm not going to fix what isn't broken,' " Brian said. "So I didn't write on this album. It doesn't matter with AC/DC. You're all together and whatever happens, happens."

The album produced two substantial hits in "Thunderstruck" and "Moneytalks." Angus explains the inspiration for the former: "I was in an airplane over East Germany, and the plane got struck by lightning. I thought my number was up. The stewardess said we were struck by lightning and I said, 'No, we were struck by thunder, because it boomed.' "

As for the latter number, Angus commented, "Money's the big divider. Other places (than America) aren't necessarily like that. In Europe, they think you've got to be born with class. [In the U.S.] they think you buy it, like it comes with the tux. So it's just our little dig at the lifestyle of the rich and faceless."

The album's atypically spooky-sounding title track found the band, uncharacteristically, stretching out. "We had the main riff, and there was something ominous about it," explained Angus. "And for that reason alone we decided to go ahead with it. In the past we'd stay away from things that sounded too musical."

"There's a lot more melody in [on *The Razors Edge*], and

we've always been wary of melody," agreed Brian. "A song like 'Moneytalks' or 'Thunderstruck,' there are real melodies in those songs . . . I had to learn again what to do with that nonsense."

By now, rock critics—once the band's mortal enemies—tended to be appreciative of AC/DC's history and long-standing refusal to compromise its basic musical values. As Craig Tomashoff wrote in *People,* "The band never gets so carried away with speed and volume that it forgets to throw in a catchy pop hook to keep things interesting. There are actual songs here, not wads of noise."

Indeed, by this point AC/DC's hardheaded adherence to its original principles had earned the respect of many a critic. As Jim Washburn wrote in the *Los Angeles Times,* "At a time when most other alloyed outfits are doing clone-like 'sensitive' semi-acoustic ballads—requisite now that market researchers have determined they need them to woo the female buyers—the Youngs and co. do nothing but hard-driving rock, with the subjects ranging from rocking all night to rocking all night."

In addition to selling 8 million copies worldwide, *The Razors Edge* restored AC/DC to the upper reaches of the *Billboard* charts after a long absence. The album reached number 2, with only pop-rapper M. C. Hammer keeping the band from the top slot. Typically, the band took its comeback in stride.

By now, it was obvious that video—a medium that AC/DC had avoided until it no longer could—had played an important role in restoring the band to the top, and the band's history of outrageously witty mini-movies continued with the clip that director David Mallet shot for "Thunderstruck." The video, filmed at London's Brixton Academy, was one of the band's most elaborate to date, successfully mixing earthy humor with high-tech production values, featuring performance footage shot on a stage with a clear Plexiglas floor (through which the camera captured Angus's fancy footwork from the bottom up) and a cast of approximately one thousand fans hanging from overhead girders.

"It was a really exciting thing to be part of," Brian said of the video shoot in an interview with the *St. Louis Post-Dispatch.* "David Mallet ran a couple of spots on the radio the morning of the shoot, and more than a thousand kids showed up . . . I believe [the sound of the band was] only just equal to the sound of those thousand voices chanting along."

"Moneytalks" was accompanied by a video featuring thousands of fake dollar bills bearing Angus's likeness. The Angus bucks were also a feature of AC/DC's 1990 tour, on which every night piles of the bogus bills showered audiences during "Moneytalks." The tour—with Malcolm Young back in the saddle—also saw the band, whose live presentation had once been as spartan as its songs, once again upping the ante on its concert presentation, using a sleekly futuristic, multileveled, red-neon-trimmed stage.

The 153-date *Razors Edge* tour, during which AC/DC played for over 3 million fans in twenty-one countries, was one of the biggest and most successful of the band's career, running from late 1989 though the early months of 1991, while America was deep in the spell of Gulf War mania—which Angus acknowledged by dropping his drawers to reveal stars-and-stripes boxer shorts. The two-and-a-half-hour shows began with "Thunderstruck," signaled by rumblings of mock thunder and lightning that flashed to reveal Angus. By the third song, "Back in Black," the lights revealed the three-tiered metal cellblock at the back of the stage, which Johnson would later climb to sing "Jailbreak." The set also featured elaborate lighting rigs and ramps, the better to highlight Angus's gyrations. Other stage frills, along with the by-now-standard bell and cannons, included cartoonish inflatable heads bearing the likeness of both Angus and the devil. Near the end of the show, Angus materialized on a platform in the middle of the arena to play a solo. Meanwhile, at the merchandise stands, official AC/DC panties could be had for a mere twelve dollars.

Despite the show's visual accoutrements, the band's essential focus was unchanged. Reviewing a November show, *Toronto Star* critic Mitch Potter pointed out, "Angus was the show, cupping hand over ear between every lick in mock disappointment, taunting his fans for response, racing from runway to runway in a giddy gumbooted twist on Chuck Berry's duckwalk, even dropping his drawers at one point (another pair was underneath) in a particularly silly striptease . . . In the grand scheme of hard rock, you are unlikely to come across a more likable delinquent than Angus," Potter observed. "[He] still wears those ridiculous public school short pants that good-naturedly debunked the Axe God myth back in the late '70s."

Potter also presented a possible explanation for the band's longevity and its recent resurgence. "Could it be that the latest wave of hard rock is so pitifully dull that tried-and-true vets like AC/DC win crowds by default?"

By this point, AC/DC's proudly untrendy approach had taken on the air of a crusade, providing a staunchly basic, proudly unfashionable alternative to the mannered, manicured power-ballad-laden beauty contest that the hard-rock genre had largely become. As the *Orlando Sentinel* wrote in a February review of an AC/DC show at the Orlando Arena, "No spandex here. The band doesn't lack for showmanship, however. Young was antic, duck-walking across the stage like Chuck Berry having leg spasms, and sprinting up the ramps at either side of the stage front. Several times he threw himself down on the raised platforms in a guitar-torturing tantrum, lying on his back and bucking against the floor as he played. The sturdily built Johnson frequently yielded center stage, but maintained his powerful presence, sinking into a fighter's crouch to emit those penetrating screams."

Reviewing the band's December show at the Long Beach Arena show in the *Los Angeles Times,* Jonathan Gold stated, "Some lead guitarists might project the image of gods, but [Angus] is the hard-rock everyman—he's the Bart Simpson of rock 'n' roll, and every teen-age boy in the audience secretly thinks he could do the same if he owned a really good electric guitar and his brother was a famous record producer." Gold also gave high marks to the returned Malcolm: "It's his chunky, mildly syncopated riffs that make the band so immediately identifiable."

Chris Slade was a fine addition to the band's backline, thumping no less than three bass drums to power the band's underrated rhythmic attack. As Jonathan Gold observed, "In the way that AC/DC's thumping, foursquare beat makes even the simplest syncopations swing way funky—which is why idiot-simple AC/DC songs rock so much harder than the most complex Red Hot Chili Peppers riffs—the band's gray stage presence sets off Angus Young's brilliance all the more clearly."

But while the band was in the midst of its biggest career high since the days of *Back in Black* and *For Those About to Rock,* tragedy struck once again on January 18, 1991, when three fans—fourteen-year-old Curtis Child, fourteen-year-old Jimmie Boyd and nineteen-year-old Elizabeth Glausi—were crushed to death after being caught in a rush to the front of the stage at a general-admission show at Salt Lake City's Salt Palace.

In addition to opening up public dialogue once again on the controversial practice of unreserved festival seating (the same admission practice that was in force when eleven fans were killed at a 1979 Who concert at Cincinnati's Riverfront Coliseum), which is illegal in some cities, and opened up the already controversial AC/DC to more charges of irresponsibility.

It also opened them up to lawsuits. Curtis Child's father filed an $8-million suit directed at AC/DC, concert promoters and county officials. Glausi's parents later sued as well.

A security man at the venue had claimed that he attempted unsuccessfully to get AC/DC's head of security to stop the concert, but the band's management maintained that the musicians had stopped playing as soon as they were made aware of the danger. What is certain is that approximately forty-five minutes after the initial crush that fatally injured the three fans, Brian Johnson came to the edge of the stage and asked the fans in front of the stage to step back.

As journalist Charles M. Young pointed out in *Musician,* accusations that the band callously continued its set while its fans were being trampled to death simply didn't ring true. "Anyone who has ever stepped onstage," wrote Young, "knows that the spotlights are blinding and the volume deafening, so it is extremely difficult to know what is happening in an audience."

The band returned to the States that summer, hitting many of the same venues as before. Reviewing a June show at California's Irvine Meadows, the *Los Angeles Times* noted that, although the show "drew its share of bawdy and boisterous audience members, it certainly wasn't the cavalcade of evil that some religious leaders have made [AC/DC's] shows out to be. Some kids in the audience were indeed doing their best to live up to the galling recent statistics on teen drinking, but most were just having an upbeat time to the exuberant, muscular music. The tone was nothing like last year's Dio-headed metal bill at the Pacific Amphitheatre, where PCP smoke and a violent mood hung in the air."

Writing in the *Seattle Times* that June, Patrick Macdonald observed, "Sameness means stagnation for most bands, but it works for AC/DC because the group obviously enjoys what it does—there's no cynicism in its formulas. Young, a compact package of pure energy (five-foot-two, 110 pounds) is a relentless showman who energizes audiences with his electricity and drive, and lead singer Brian Johnson is a burly prole who doesn't fit the rock-star mold."

Not surprisingly, Brian Johnson had a simpler explanation: "We play the music we feel. We've never viewed ourselves as great artists—just as five blokes who enjoy getting together and playing some music."

"We play as a unit," said Angus. "I think that's why we are what we are. We get out there, and we don't try and go crazy. I mean, I'm standing out there jumping around a lot, but it's more nervous energy than anything. Same with Brian. We've always been pretty out front, and we always went onstage with that attitude. We always said, 'If you're gonna do something, make sure you let 'em know you're doing it, y'know!'

"We've never tried to say we're better than our audience," insisted Angus. "There's a lot of people who come to see us and go, 'I can do what he does.' I've never said to an audience, 'You're going to have to applaud 'cause we're here, so stand up and go nuts.' AC/DC knows when we go onstage, we go to work."

"We have the best jobs in the world," Brian gushed. "Millions of people love us everywhere we go, and we get to visit them whenever we want to tour. We'd have to be even dumber than we are to give that up. I know that some bands have internal problems that make life very difficult, but nothing could be less true where we're concerned; we love each other like brothers."

One member of the AC/DC family, however, did not live to appreciate the full impact of the group's 1990 comeback. Early mentor Ted Albert, whose production company and publishing concern had been instrumental in the band's rise to prominence, died of cancer that year.

27

GET IT HOT

Despite the Salt Lake City incident and the ongoing persecution stemming from it, AC/DC topped off what had basically been a ragingly successful touring campaign by topping the bill at the eleventh Monsters of Rock festival at Castle Donington, gaining the distinction of being the only band to headline the fest three times. Sharing the bill this year were such luminaries as Metallica, Motley Crüe, the Black Crowes and Queensryche.

"That was just amazing," said Brian Johnson, who at some point during the Donington show reportedly told Motley Crüe's Nikki Sixx that his tattoos looked as if someone had thrown up on his arm. "This isn't all about money; that sort of recognition from your professional mates and then the crowd reaction, it was too much. We're really proud and grateful at the same time."

The following month, on September 28, 1991, the Monsters

of Rock tag was tied to a somewhat more prestigious and historic gig, a precedent-setting multi-act concert in the former Soviet Union, at Moscow's Tushino Airfield, where AC/DC headlined a ten-hour extravaganza that also included Metallica, the Black Crowes, Pantera and a local group chosen by the votes of Russian fans. The show drew a crowd officially estimated at 150,000, though other estimates ran considerably higher.

"The military stopped counting at 850,000," a typically hyperbolic Angus later claimed to the *Boston Globe*'s Steve Morse. "And when we went on, they said that people were still coming in. The city was empty. It seemed that everyone was at the concert."

Angus further stated that a potential international incident was narrowly avoided when the band pulled out its cannons on "For Those About to Rock." "When the military heard the cannons, they really freaked," he said. "You saw their mouths drop. You almost heard them say, 'We've been tricked! It's a dirty imperialist trick!' "

The concert was presented as a "celebration of democracy and freedom" staged as a gift to Russian youth for their resistance against the recent failed military coup. "It happened just thirty days after the coup attempt and it was the Moscow government's way of saying thank you to the kids for helping stop the coup," said Brian. "It was inspiring seeing these kids who'd put their lives on the line, rocking out to AC/DC like kids anywhere."

The Moscow show also represented a large-scale commercial venture for its American corporate sponsor, Time Warner, Inc. The concert was televised in Russia, filmed for an as-yet-unreleased documentary by prominent music-video director Wayne Isham (there were usually twice as many camera operators onstage as musicians) and recorded for a projected live album. Though over a thousand militiamen were positioned around the stage as a security force, the rock-starved crowd was rowdy and rambunctious, with scattered arrests for unruly behavior.

"The crowd was maybe crazier than any audience we had played for," said Angus. "The government had insisted that the military be used to provide most of the security, but some of them started beating the kids with sticks. In the end, our security guys got them to pull back and just watch the show."

The Russian concert was particularly significant in light of the fact that most Western rock music was outlawed in the USSR until the rise of *glasnost*. Although AC/DC had long been popular among Soviet youth, the band's recordings could only be obtained on the black market.

Like the Moscow show, the final leg of the *Razors Edge* world tour ended on a sour note in November in Wellington, New Zealand, where two fans received stab wounds and several suffered drug overdoses. After the show, unruly fans rampaged through town damaging cars and shop windows. By the end of the day, fifty arrests had reportedly been made.

The band was a good deal more comfortable with the sort of trouble that they'd encountered in Belfast earlier in the tour, when Angus attempted his striptease bit. "I was wearing two pair of shorts," Angus recalled. "And I didn't know the pair underneath had ripped in the front. So I pull these shorts down and Malcolm's looking at me going [makes alarmed face and pointing gesture] . . . And I'm too busy in my own little world. I'm sort of thinking, 'What's he pointing at?' And the police are all sort of looking at me. And I turned around to the audience and they're all sort of stunned. And I sort of look down and there's all my wedding tackle hanging out for all the world to see.

"The audience was good about it, and, as Brian said, I've got nothing to hide!"

Further evidence that *The Razors Edge* had restored AC/DC to the top arrived in the form of a Grammy nomination in the hard-rock category, in which AC/DC was pitted against Faith No More, Jane's Addiction, Living Colour and Motley Crüe.

28

RUFF STUFF

After another break between studio albums—during which it was rumored that Angus and Malcolm contemplated firing Brian Johnson—the group released *AC/DC Live,* drawn from various shows on the lengthy *Razors Edge* tour. In an unusual move that was indicative of the recent upsurge in demand for AC/DC product, the live album was released as a fourteen-song single CD, a specially packaged twenty-three-song double CD, a twenty-three-song cassette, and an eighteen-song videocassette and laser disc, *Live at Donington.*

The video version, shot on high-quality 35-millimeter film by David Mallet, did a good job of capturing the atmosphere of the AC/DC live experience, in a manner considerably more advanced than its relatively primitive predecessor *Let There Be Rock,* thanks to Mallet's inventive use of camera angles.

As the band's second live album (not counting the numerous bootlegs that have proliferated over the years), *AC/DC*

Live demonstrated just how much—and how little—AC/DC had changed in the fourteen years since *If You Want Blood, You've Got It.*

"We wanted to capture it before the hair and the teeth drop down," Angus joked. "We didn't want to be on life support systems . . . The album really is more for the AC/DC collector. When you're talking to them at the shows, it's always the first thing—'When you guys going to do another live album?'

"Probably the most asked question of anyone in the band is, 'When are we going to get another live dose?' " said Angus. "But we wanted to wait until Brian had a lot of studio albums under his belt, so he'd get a fair shake."

AC/DC Live was drawn from various shows on the *Razors Edge* tour, including the Donington and Moscow shows, as well as shows in America, Canada and Scotland. "I'm not sure where all the songs on the live record come from," Brian admitted. "I've been so mixed up with all the tapes being sent back and forth. The songs come from Moscow, Donington, Scotland, Canada and America. They didn't want to put too much from one place because somebody would be insulted. They tried to be a bit diplomatic, but most of it is from America and Canada."

The live album was also a response to bootleggers, who over the years have released a variety of unauthorized AC/DC concert recordings, of varying levels of quality. "Many a bootlegger's captured the whole feel of an AC/DC live gig," said Angus. "So we thought maybe it's our turn. And this was the best time, because we had done a lot of touring—nearly two years."

"We're constantly being bootlegged in Europe and Asia, so we're [bootlegging] ourselves," Brian added. "Both the live double album and the video have odd songs that weren't singles or that we don't perform very often."

As for the varying formats, Angus commented, "All the band concentrated on was the double-album thing. The single album is part of a record company idea for the person who might only know us from 'Back in Black' . . . We're not trying to do a greatest hits 'cause we've never had one."

A fringe benefit of releasing a live collection, Angus pointed out, was to give the band a bit of extra time to spend on its next studio effort. "We're pretty lucky at this moment. We've got a little time to play with. The good thing about it is we can get to write a whole new record without somebody saying, 'Come on, guys, you've got two weeks to finish it!' Hopefully, we can do this next one exactly the way we want."

"Sure, it gives us a little breathing space until the next studio album comes out," said Brian. "But we didn't want to put out a stopgap record. We wanted it to be a little special, to give the fans a wide choice . . . Does putting out all this material mean we're cashing in and then packing it up? I'm being asked that and I'll tell you, definitely not."

As Angus told *Circus,* the band tried to stay away from doing too much studio tinkering on the live tracks. "There's the inevitable feedback, the squeaks, the snare drum rattle, the technical things, you try to pull all that out," he admitted. "But when it comes to a bum note . . . you know, I never hit a bum note. God forbid! I prefer to call it artistic license. If you were going to fix up that sort of thing, then it becomes a studio album."

Asked to name his own favorite in-concert discs, Angus answered, "The Allman Brothers *Live at the Fillmore*—that's a great live album. There's a couple of great tracks on *Woodstock,* like the Who doing their version of 'Summertime Blues.' The other live album by the Who, *Live at Leeds,* is great, and so is B.B. King *Live at Cook County Jail.* Another great one for me was a Muddy Waters thing. Just after he passed away they released a live album with Johnny Winter doing a lot of the guitar."

The fact that *AC/DC Live* became the band's biggest seller since *For Those About to Rock* suggested that the band members weren't lying when they claimed to still feel in touch with their young fans. "I was young once!" insisted Angus. "I still walk around the streets. It's not like we're cut off. There's always plenty of young people who want to come and talk to you . . . And we're not the hardest act to get to meet. If you hang on any street corner, you're likely to see one of us if we're in town."

29

HELL OR HIGH WATER

The various versions of *AC/DC Live* did a fine job of consolidating the group's comeback. The album's new version of "Highway to Hell" was even nominated for a Best Hard Rock Performance Grammy, alongside tracks by Living Colour, Robert Plant, Smashing Pumpkins and Stone Temple Pilots.

Elsewhere, the band's enduring status as a cultural icon was underlined by such prominent signifiers as the AC/DC T-shirt invariably worn by animated teen imbecile Butthead on MTV's controversial *Beavis and Butthead* series, and by the success of numerous regional AC/DC "tribute" bands with names like Hell's Bells, Back in Black and Long Gon Bon, specializing in faithful reproductions of the band's repertoire as well as Angus's stage moves.

Despite their restored prominence, all that was heard from AC/DC between 1993 and 1995 was the high-caliber "Big Gun," the band's contribution to the sound track of the Arnold

Schwarzenegger extravaganza *The Last Action Hero*. The hugely expensive film proved to be a monumental flop, but its sound track album (also featuring tracks by Alice in Chains, Queensryche, Anthrax, Def Leppard, Megadeth, Tesla, Fishbone and Cypress Hill) was considerably more successful, thanks in part to "Big Gun"—which, as the disc's lead track and first single, was accompanied by a promo video combining footage of AC/DC with filmed vignettes featuring Schwarzenegger. Still, *Entertainment Weekly* dismissed the disc as "a sludge-metal scrap pile" and AC/DC's contribution as "weak."

"Big Gun" was also significant in that it marked the band's first teaming with young producer/entrepreneur Rick Rubin. Rubin had gotten his start as a partner in the influential New York rap label Def Jam (rap being another musical style that the Young brothers openly despised) and had subsequently launched the more rock-oriented Def American label. Rubin's hands-off production approach had helped to revitalize the recording careers of veteran artists as diverse as Aerosmith, Tom Petty and Johnny Cash. As a long-standing fan, Rubin was eager to work with the band, and "Big Gun" served as a road test for a more substantial collaboration on the next AC/DC album.

By now, the band's creative cycle had been altered by the process of its members growing up and growing apart. When not on the road or in the studio, they're scattered geographically, Angus in the Netherlands with wife Ellen; Malcolm and Chris in England; and Cliff and the remarried Brian in Florida. "It's a lot easier to get from point A to B," Angus points out. "Sometimes it's easier, if I'm in Europe, to go to New York than fly to London. Travel is just faster these days.

"Once you start the process of saying, 'All right, we're

recording now,' you're more or less together for three years," Angus continues. "It's like an intense marriage. You need those little breaks afterward, so you can look forward to getting back together again. And when you do, it's like you've never left. There's just that bond. Everyone talks to each other. We've never had an attitude problem. You're all together as one little team and you have to get along.

"What usually happens is I say, 'All right, I've got enough material,' then I give [Malcolm] a call and he says, 'Well, give me another week.' Then we get together and sift through everything we've got and pick out the best. That's how we've always done it. The writing can be anyplace, sometimes even on the road. Or sometimes we might come straight off the road, play each other ideas, work out what we want to do, then say, 'See you next record.' "

30

HARD AS A ROCK

By the end of 1995, the music industry had seen the commercial ascendance of numerous unapologetically noisy "alternative" bands, whose mainstream success had opened the American airwaves up to the sort of loud, raw noise that had long been anathema to commercial rock-radio programmers. Many of these bands openly acknowledged AC/DC's influence, with none of the grudging respect that had once routinely accompanied such citations. Indeed, it seemed as if AC/DC was more widely loved than ever.

In light of the atmosphere of renewed interest, the release of *BallBreaker*—the first new AC/DC studio album in five years—was especially timely. Its release was preceded by a promotional trip to New York, where the band received an award acknowledging their worldwide sales of more than 80 million records.

One indicator of AC/DC's newly hip cachet was the involvement of the new album's producer, rap/metal mover-and-shaker Rick Rubin, who'd apparently passed his audition with "Big Gun." "He's been an AC/DC fan since he was a little kid in New York, and he loves the early stuff," Malcolm said of Rubin, who was assisted in the studio by longtime AC/DC cohort Mike Fraser. "He told us one of the first tracks he'd ever done with a rap group was 'Highway to Hell'!"

"My first impressions of Rick Rubin was this big guy, twice my height, with sunglasses, lying on the floor doing yoga and telling us what a big AC/DC fan he was!" added Angus.

"He's more of a fan than a producer," commented Brian. "So it was like having another pair of ears—which is what you need when you're making an album. I think the songs on this album ended up sounding more like the old AC/DC than anything we'd done since *For Those About to Rock.*"

Perhaps even more unexpected than the teaming of Rubin and AC/DC was the return of Phil Rudd, who'd exited the AC/DC camp a decade prior, and who'd pretty much retired from life as a professional musician. According to the band's press bio, he'd been "flying helicopters in New Zealand."

"We hadn't seen Phil in about ten years," said Malcolm, "so when we were playing in New Zealand, we thought we'd give him a call. He seemed just like the old Phil. Then, around May (of 1994), me and Angus were jamming and we just said, 'Let's jam with the guy and see how it goes.' We'd already decided that musically we wanted to try to get back to where we were on the old records, and Phil was the missing ingredient."

The band had begun work on *BallBreaker* with the stated objective of returning to the unfussed simplicity of its early recordings, but that goal proved a bit more difficult than anticipated.

It started off innocently enough. "Malcolm called me up and said, 'How are you doing there? I'm bored! Got plenty of ideas. Shall we get going then?' " Angus recounted. "It's always pretty much like that. We always seem to know when we've had enough of a break. Though it wasn't as long a break as some people seem to think. We got together and jammed, and the songs seemed to just fall into place."

Unfortunately, the album's birth cycle was plagued by a series of delays. The band spent ten weeks in a New York studio trying to capture proper vibe, before scrapping everything they'd recorded and moving the project to Los Angeles.

"We jammed a lot this time," said Malcolm. "And because of the delays in the studio, we jammed even more! I'd say we were together almost a year just playing, making this album. Things got really tight—sort of thing you usually only get on tour. So that gave us a great vibe in the studio. We want our albums to sound like our best live gigs, and normally you have to shut your eyes and imagine you're back onstage again. But this time we were already in the stage mode."

According to Johnson, the five months the band spent recording in L.A. were "brilliant. We were having such a good time I didn't want to go home! When we all first got together, it's always fun, because you haven't got a clue what is going to happen next. The boys just come in with some riffs—I don't know where they get them from, they're brilliant—and all I have to do is open my mouth and shout my tits off. And I don't even have to pay to get into the gigs!"

Despite the album's bumpy road to completion, the end result more than justified the production hassles. The infectiously rhythmic "Hard as a Rock" opens the album with an uncharacteristically jangly guitar hook that gives way to some furious testifying from Brian Johnson. "Cover You in Oil," "Hail Caesar" and "Love Bomb" offer driving melody lines to match their pared-down sound, while "The Honey Roll," "The Furor" and "Whiskey on the Rocks" possess a down-and-dirty blues/funk vibe recalling the *Powerage* era. The blooze-inflected "Boogie Man" found Johnson stretching out in a manner that, at least momentarily, recalled Angus's childhood idol, Louis Armstrong. Stranger still, "Burnin' Alive" seemed to hint at—heaven forbid—oblique political comment, but Brian screamed loudly enough that fans probably didn't notice.

The title track, according to Malcolm, "was the last song we wrote, and it came together real quick. We just thought of the hardest and heaviest thing we could, and it came from there and just seemed to sum the whole album up."

"I'm really proud of this album," concluded Angus. "I can honestly say I love every one of the songs—and that's something, coming from a band that started just after the Crucifixion."

Even before *BallBreaker* had been released to the public, the band seemed to be basking in a mood of renewal, speaking excitedly of taking on new challenges. "We want to go everywhere, even places no man or woman has boldly gone before," said Angus. "[Now that] the Wall has come down, there's more and more places to play in the East. And Asia's opening up more and more, and it wants its slab of Western culture—and who better to do it than AC/DC!"

As for the breakup rumors and whisperings of interband strife that now seemed to precede every AC/DC album, Malcolm took them in stride. "We've been going so long [that] they always say that. No, we're gonna keep on rocking. We don't know any better!"

Similarly, rumors that Angus had considered abandoning his schoolboy persona were greeted with amusement by their subject's brother. "Angus *is* the schoolboy," said Malcolm. "He changes when he gets into his uniform. He's not my kid brother anymore; he's wild. No, I know Angus too well, and

I couldn't see him up there in an Armani suit like Eric Clapton!"

To accompany *BallBreaker*'s first single, "Hard as a Rock," the band shot another good-naturedly elaborate video—their seventh collaboration with director David Mallet. For the occasion, four hundred London-area AC/DC fans—recruited via radio and the Internet grapevine—were driven by bus to a soundstage at Bray Studios in Windsor, best known as the location where such classic Hammer horror films as *The Curse of Frankenstein* and *The Horror of Dracula* were shot.

Angus spent much of the shoot hanging in midair on a giant demolition ball, on which he eventually came crashing through a window amidst a hail of candy-glass shrapnel and exploding fireworks. "It's scary!" Angus fretted. "I'm not that brave, and they don't pay me any extra for it! My whole life was flashing before me up there! David Mallet is always coming up with these crazy schemes to try and kill me!"

As if such high-concept, high-tech video shenanigans weren't enough to make it clear that the Highway to Hell had finally merged with the Information Superhighway, the Ariola Interactive Entertainment division of BMG Australia announced a multi-band AC/DC tribute CD that would integrate interactive CD-ROM visuals as well as new versions of classic AC/DC tunes recorded by young Australian bands. The album's most radical reinterpretation was an impassioned reading of "Jailbreak," by the eclectic Australian combo Yothu Yindi, which mixed rock instruments with elements of traditional Aboriginal music.

Angus prepares for liftoff. (David Corio, Retna)

31

RIDE ON

As much as AC/DC has grown, certain things haven't changed. For one thing, there's the Young brothers' deeply ingrained suspicion of political causes. "I don't believe in it," Angus says. "Take your 'Save the Trees' issue. I mean, my guitar is made of wood. A tree's been chopped down to make that guitar. I'd be a hypocrite 'cause I've got about twenty-one of those bits of wood. That's probably one tree in itself. Every rock 'n' roll musician's got a wooden guitar, including Sting. It's hypocritical.

"We are there as a rock 'n' roll band to give fun and entertainment," Angus continued. "And we don't want to go out there and bullshit an audience. An audience can smell bullshit from a fuckin' mile away. It might wash once but when you come on twice, be prepared for the ripe tomato. When we started in the clubs our attitude was, we had one intention—rock 'n' roll! And we go for the same thing now . . . AC/DC never got sidetracked, to go this way or that way. We know what we do best, we play rock music.

"I never take it seriously. Rock 'n' roll music was meant to be fun. I pick up a guitar and play it for enjoyment. If somebody says to me, do you think you're alienating an audience, are you being sexist, are you being this, are you being that? Are you doing harm to anyone out there? Hey, that's the last thing on my mind. The first thing is to get out there and have fun."

"We're just pranksters more than anything," says Brian. "You're having fun. And that's all there is. If a kid thinks he's being naughty by singing 'Highway to Hell,' great, because all he's doing is singing or chanting or putting his arms in the air. It's not meant to harm anyone. It's not like I'm coming out with my personal views and [the] meaning of life. If you do that, you're in the same baseball game as those religious fanatics, or those English bands who hop on a cause, any cause, just to get themselves a bit of publicity."

Asked to predict AC/DC's long-term future, Angus has a ready answer. "I don't think I could walk on that stage and do what I do or any of the lads do if we couldn't be honest," Angus insisted. "If it all went bad, we would feel it more than anyone. I couldn't get out there and rip people off in any shape or form. If there's one thing I believe in, then, it's that. If you're not going to be honest in what you do, then you might as well fucking give up."

By the 1990s AC/DC's status as an institution was solidly established, the band having won the rock establishment's respect through sheer stubbornness and perseverance. But the band seemed intent on maintaining its rebellious gutter aura, as Angus told *Circus.* "As soon as they start liking you, I think then you've got a problem . . . We've never been one to make yourself look nice or pretty or acceptable.

"This DJ came into our dressing room and said, 'Hi, I'm so-and-so from so-and-so, I used to listen to your albums a few years ago and, to be honest with you, I didn't like them, but these kids kept ringing up and requesting them and gradually I've grown to like it.' And I just said to him, 'Pal, with us you either like it or hate it and if you didn't like it then I'll be buggered if you like it now.' I just told him what I thought and showed him the door."

"We've just kept plugging away at what we do," Angus told *Spin.* "I know that sounds like a simple answer, but I've never tried to write songs for any particular reason than to do what I like and think is good. Yeah, there's a lot of people out there who write music they think other people will like or what they're told other people will like, and then those people end up wondering why they're not successful at it. If we'd tried to write songs for those reasons, we'd probably be unemployed alongside those people. Luckily, we've been able to keep doing it, and hopefully it'll continue for a while."

"We've never pulled any punches," added Brian. "We just play music that's fun and simple—the way our audience likes it. We're not gonna write some real serious political stuff that has no meaning to us—leave that for someone else to do. We're not here to save the world, we're here to play rock music. That's what we do, and that's why we're still around."

"A lot has happened since our days with Bon," says Angus. "But at the same time, I don't think music's really changed that much over the years. It's still all about making good music and the fans liking it. The business side of it hasn't really changed too much either—there's still the same kind of problems to deal with. You always hear about how all these revivals or new trends are taking place, but as far as I'm concerned, we're just trying to do what we're good at."

Now settled into stable family lives, the Young brothers and their bandmates nonetheless show no signs of losing their original fervor. Though AC/DC has long since left its native Australia, its rock 'n' roll fire remains undimmed and its enthusiasm for the future seems as strong as ever.

"AC/DC has survived because we've never changed direction, never given in to trends," Brian told the *Toronto Star*. "That's why there haven't been any solo projects from within the band. No one's ever wanted to. Our music doesn't go out of fashion because it isn't about fashion. I hear about all these different kinds of music: grunge, hardcore, death metal. And all it is is rock 'n' roll.

"Our music comes from the heart," concluded the singer. "It's always been there. People put ya down for playin' rock 'n' roll, you know. Well, fuck those people. You got to do your own thing."

32

THAT'S THE WAY I WANNA ROCK 'N' ROLL

AC/DC ALBUM DISCOGRAPHY

HIGH VOLTAGE, 1975
Produced by Harry Vanda
and George Young
Baby, Please Don't Go;
She's Got Balls; Little Lover;
Stick Around; Soul Stripper;
You Ain't Got a Hold on
Me; Love Song; Show
Business

TNT, 1976
Produced by Harry Vanda
and George Young
It's a Long Way to the Top
(If You Wanna Rock 'n'
Roll); Rock 'n' Roll Singer;
The Jack; Live Wire; T.N.T.;
Rocker; Can I Sit Next to
You Girl; High Voltage;
School Day

HIGH VOLTAGE
(U.S./British version),
1976
Produced by Harry Vanda
and George Young
It's a Long Way to the Top
(If You Wanna Rock 'n'
Roll); Rock 'n' Roll Singer;
The Jack; Live Wire; T.N.T.;

Can I Sit Next to You Girl;
Little Lover; She's Got Balls;
High Voltage

DIRTY DEEDS DONE DIRT CHEAP, 1976
Produced by Harry Vanda
and George Young
Dirty Deeds Done Dirt
Cheap; Ain't No Fun
(Waiting Around to Be a
Millionaire); There's Gonna
Be Some Rockin'; Problem
Child; Squealer; Big Balls;
Rock in Peace; Ride On;
Jailbreak

LET THERE BE ROCK, 1977
Produced by Harry Vanda
and George Young
Go Down; Dog Eat Dog; Let
There Be Rock; Bad Boy
Boogie; Problem Child;
Overdose; Hell Ain't a Bad
Place to Be; Whole Lotta
Rosie

POWERAGE, 1978
Produced by Harry Vanda
and George Young
Rock 'n' Roll Damnation;
Down Payment Blues;
Gimme a Bullet; Riff Raff;
Sin City; What's Next to the
Moon; Gone Shootin'; Up to
My Neck in You; Kicked in
the Teeth

IF YOU WANT BLOOD, YOU'VE GOT IT, 1978
Produced by Harry Vanda
and George Young
Riff Raff; Hell Ain't a Bad
Place to Be; Bad Boy Boogie;
The Jack; Problem Child;
Whole Lotta Rosie; Rock 'n'
Roll Damnation; High
Voltage; Let There Be Rock;
Rocker

HIGHWAY TO HELL, 1979
Produced by Robert John
"Mutt" Lange
Highway to Hell; Girls Got
Rhythm; Walk All Over
You; Touch Too Much;
Beating Around the Bush;
Shot Down in Flames; Get It
Hot; If You Want Blood
(You've Got It); Love
Hungry Man; Night Prowler

BACK IN BLACK, 1980
Produced by Robert John
"Mutt" Lange
Hells Bells; Shoot to Thrill;
What Do You Do for Money
Honey; Given the Dog a
Bone; Let Me Put My Love
Into You; Back in Black;
You Shook Me All Night
Long; Have a Drink on Me;
Shake a Leg; Rock and Roll
Ain't Noise Pollution

DIRTY DEEDS DONE
DIRT CHEAP (U.S.
version), 1980
Produced by Harry Vanda
and George Young
Dirty Deeds Done Dirt
Cheap; Love at First Feel;
Big Balls; Rocker; Problem
Child; There's Gonna Be
Some Rockin'; Ain't No Fun
(Waiting Around to Be a
Millionaire); Ride On;
Squealer

FOR THOSE ABOUT
TO ROCK, WE SALUTE
YOU, 1981
Produced by Robert John
"Mutt" Lange
For Those About to Rock

(We Salute You); Put the
Finger on You; Let's Get It
Up; Inject the Venom;
Snowballed; Evil Walks;
C.O.D.; Breaking the Rules;
Night of the Long Knives;
Spellbound

FLICK OF THE
SWITCH, 1983
Produced by AC/DC
Rising Power; This House Is
on Fire; Flick of the Switch;
Nervous Shakedown;
Landslide; Guns for Hire;
Deep in the Hole; Bedlam in
Belgium; Badlands; Brain
Shake

'74 JAILBREAK, 1984
Produced by Harry Vanda
and George Young
Jailbreak; You Ain't Got a
Hold on Me; Show Business;
Soul Stripper; Baby, Please
Don't Go

FLY ON THE WALL,
1985
Produced by Angus Young
and Malcolm Young
Fly on the Wall; Shake Your
Foundations; First Blood;

Danger; Sink the Pink;
Playing With Girls; Stand
Up; Hell or High Water;
Back in Business; Send for
the Man

WHO MADE WHO, 1986
Various tracks produced by
Harry Vanda and George
Young; Robert John "Mutt
Lange; Angus Young and
Malcolm Young
Who Made Who; You Shook
Me All Night Long; D.T.;
Sink the Pink; Ride On;
Hells Bells; Shake Your
Foundations; Chase the Ace;
For Those About to Rock
(We Salute You)

BLOW UP YOUR VIDEO, 1988
Produced by Harry Vanda
and George Young
Heatseeker; That's the Way I
Wanna Rock 'n' Roll;
Meanstreak; Go Zone;
Kissin' Dynamite; Nick of
Time; Some Sin for Nuthin';
Ruff Stuff; Two's Up; This
Means War

THE RAZORS EDGE, 1990
Produced by Bruce Fairbairn
Thunderstruck; Fire Your
Guns; Moneytalks; The
Razors Edge; Mistress for
Christmas; Rock Your Heart
Out; Are You Ready; Got
You by the Balls; Shot of
Love; Lets Make It;
Goodbye & Good Riddance
to Bad Luck; If You Dare

AC/DC LIVE (complete version), 1992
Produced by Bruce Fairbairn
Thunderstruck; Shoot to
Thrill; Back in Black; Sin
City; Who Made Who;
Heatseeker; Fire Your
Guns; Jailbreak; The Jack;
The Razors Edge; Dirty
Deeds Done Dirt Cheap;
Moneytalks; Hells Bells; Are
You Ready; That's the Way
I Wanna Rock 'n' Roll;
High Voltage; You Shook
Me All Night Long; Whole
Lotta Rosie; Let There Be
Rock; Bonny; Highway to
Hell; T.N.T.; For Those
About to Rock (We Salute
You)

AC/DC LIVE (abridged version), 1992
Produced by Bruce Fairbairn
Thunderstruck; Shoot to Thrill; Back in Black; Who Made Who; Heatseeker; The Jack; Moneytalks; Hells Bells; Dirty Deeds Done Dirt Cheap; Whole Lotta Rosie; You Shook Me All Night Long; Highway to Hell; T.N.T.; For Those About to Rock (We Salute You)

BALLBREAKER, 1995
Produced by Rick Rubin
Hard as a Rock; Cover You in Oil; The Furor; Boogie Man; The Honey Roll; Burnin' Alive; Hail Caesar; Love Bomb; Caught With Your Pants Down; Whiskey on the Rocks; Ballbreaker